Images of Nebuchadnezzar

Images of Nebuchadnezzar

The Emergence of a Legend

Ronald H. Sack

SUP

Selinsgrove: Susquehanna University Press
London and Toronto: Associated University Presses

Associated University Presses
440 Forsgate Drive
Cranbury, NJ 08512

Associated University Presses
25 Sicilian Avenue
London WC1A 2QH, England

Associated University Presses
P.O. Box 39, Clarkson Pstl. Stn.
Mississauga, Ontario,
L5J 3X9 Canada

The paper used in this publication meets the requirements
of the American National Standard for Permanence of Paper
for Printed Library Materials Z39.48-1984.

Library of Congress Cataloging-in-Publication Data

Sack, Ronald Herbert.
    Images of Nebuchadnezzar : the emergence of a legend / Ronald H. Sack.
        p. cm.
    Includes bibliographical references and index.
    ISBN 0-945636-35-0 (alk. paper)
    1. Nebuchadnezzar II King of Babylonia, d. 562 B.C. 2. Babylonia--
History--Sources. 3. Babylonia--Kings and rulers--Biography.
    I. Title.
DS73.92.S23 1991
935'.04'092--dc20
    [B]   91-55023
                                                           CIP

PRINTED IN THE UNITED STATES OF AMERICA

For

Sarah, Dan, and Mike

Contents

Preface

With the capture of Babylon by Cyrus II of Persia in 539 B.C., the eleventh Babylonian dynasty came to an end. Founded by the Chaldean sheikh Nabopolassar (Akk Nabû-apla-usur) on 23 November 626 B.C., this period witnessed some of the more significant events in the history of the ancient Near East. However, despite the plethora of letters, economic contract tablets, building inscriptions, and chronicles surviving the age, large gaps in our knowledge of the Chaldean period from primary sources still exist. Consequently, historians must utilize descriptions of a number of these events in secondary sources written in languages other than Akkadian. The conquest of the Jews and their subsequent deportation by Nebuchadnezzar, the building of imposing walls around Babylon, and the sojourn of Nabonidus in Tema were all noteworthy items to historians and chronographers representing a number of different value systems. Many of these sources emphasize the importance of actual historical events through the creation of a somewhat mythical picture of the individual being described. In fashioning such an image, the classical, medieval, or Hebrew author preserves a cultural attitude toward a particular person in accordance with his peculiar achievements, real or imagined. Such attitudes enable the investigation of historical periods from several different perspectives.

More than fifty years ago, Tabouis published an extensive study of *Nebuchadnezzar* (McGraw Hill, 1931) in which he attempted to incorporate some of the source material surviving from ancient times. Considering the length of the king's reign and the wealth of secondary literature contained in the books of the Old Testament, his choice of topic seems only logical. However, although the assyriologists V. Schiel, J. Strassmaier, and T. G. Pinches, among others, had already discovered and translated hundreds of cuneiform documents datable to the Chaldean period, none of them could corroborate much of the information to be found in the books of Kings, Jeremiah, and especially Daniel. Tabouis's task, therefore, of writing a biography of Nebuchadnezzar was made doubly difficult. In the light of these circumstances, it is amazing that he produced as extensive a study as he did.

Many years later, in 1956, D. J. Wiseman published a cuneiform document that has provided historians with valuable evidence concerning the first eleven years of Nebuchadnezzar's reign. For the first time, a Babylonian chronicle confirmed the siege of Jerusalem in 597 B.C. prophesied by Jeremiah. However, the tablet is broken at a crucial point and, thus far, very few other cuneiform texts have been able to tell us anything of the important events that may have taken place in southern Mesopotamia during the years 594-548 B.C. Nevertheless, Wiseman recently attempted a synthesis of all surviving evidence pertaining to Nebuchadnezzar. His important *Nebuchadrezzar and Babylon* (Oxford, 1985) includes not only a detailed biographical sketch of the most famous of Chaldean monarchs, but also presents new important archaeological evidence concerning many building projects undertaken in Babylon during the king's reign. In view of the publication of this study, it might seem unnecessary, even redundant, to probe the subject further. However, an important element clearly lacking in Wiseman's latest volume is a detailed treatment of the secondary sources (composed long after Nebuchadnezzar's death) and the cultural attitudes they reflect. Historians, for better or worse, are forced again to probe the Hebrew, Arabic, Greek, and Latin secondary sources (as well as the dated cuneiform contract tablets) in the hope of determining what actually happened during this period. Sources of this nature, when taken together, sometimes can paint intriguing pictures, accurate or not, of periods and personalities about which relatively little has been written.

I undertook the following study primarily to examine the nature of all surviving source material related to Nebuchadnezzar. It does not, therefore, pretend to be a cultural history of the Chaldean period or an all-inclusive political commentary on the reign of Nebuchadnezzar. Furthermore, while the focus of the work is on the most famous of the Chaldean monarchs, it does not treat him in a vacuum. Sources for the reign of Nabonidus (Akk Nabû-na'id), king of Babylon from 555-539 B.C. also must be included. Both of these reigns are interesting, because literally nothing is included in the surviving sources mentioning either king that might provide insight into the significant political happenings of the sixth century B.C. On the other hand, numerous cuneiform, Greek, Latin, Hebrew, and even Arabic commentaries of a secondary nature survive and appear to preserve peculiar popular traditions associated with both men. Thus the following chapters will attempt an analysis of the "image" of Nebuchadnezzar through an examination of these traditions. This approach is especially worthwhile, because many of the Greek, Latin, Arabic, and Hebrew sources have yet to be analyzed. The result will be   (1) an examination of the possible connection between the contemporary cuneiform sources for these figures and the legendary material found in other cultures, and (2) an analysis of the relationship between early written and oral traditions and the later material about Nebuchadnezzar and Nabonidus to be found in the classical and Hebrew sources. In other words, we are interested not only in what Nebuchadnezzar actually did but also in who historians or chroniclers representing a number of complex value systems *thought* the king really was.

In presenting this study, it is my intention to appeal to two separate audiences. First, I hope to acquaint the student of ancient history in general with both the varied sources for the reign of Nebuchadnezzar and the difficulties encountered in interpreting their contents. Because these sources were written in different parts of the ancient world over several centuries, numerous problems arose in transmitting information from one source to another. A somewhat technical discussion of these problems, therefore, must be included here. Hence, this investigation will also attempt to appeal to the specialists in Assyriology and Old Testament studies, because it will analyze the nature of Chaldean cuneiform sources and propose conclusions as to how and why their contents were preserved by various cultures in later times.

Several years ago, I was indeed fortunate to have been a participant in a seminar sponsored by the National Endowment for the Humanities in which the possible connections between written and oral traditions in the ancient Near East were examined. Under the able guidance of the seminar's director, Dr. Jack M. Sasson of the Department of Religion at the University of North Carolina, Chapel Hill, I completed a study of Nebuchadnezzar and Nabonidus upon which this book has been largely based. Since that time, the penetrating monograph *In Search of History* by John van Seters and William H. McNeill's collection of essays entitled *Mythistory* have appeared to further stimulate the completion of this work. As a consequence, some sections of the following chapters, in particular the Introduction, are somewhat "general" in their content. However, an overview of the area and period is essential before we focus on the specific character of Nebuchadnezzar. Fortunately, numerous colleagues have cast their critical eyes on the following chapters and have provided valuable suggestions which helped me to improve this study. I am, obviously, greatly indebted to all who helped in this way, and I sincerely hope, thanks to the generous assistance of these individuals, that this study has realized the objectives outlined above.

1
Introduction

And it shall come to pass, when seventy years are accomplished, that I will punish the king of Babylon, and that nation, saith the Lord, for their iniquity, and the land of the Chaldeans, and will make it perpetual desolations.

— Jeremiah 25:12

In 539 B.C., the city of Babylon surrendered to the armies of Cyrus the Great of Persia. Within a year, the Jews were on their way back to Palestine. The Chaldean kingdom had fallen; the Babylonian Captivity had come to an end.[1] Yet these events did not erase the memory of the previous fifty years from men's minds. Instead, they inspired literature that would forever preserve accounts of five decades of sorrow and of the monarch responsible for them. The detail included in these stories was extensive—and for good reason. The tales themselves were didactic; as such, they were handed down from generation to generation and passed on from one culture to another. Their authors, then, had to create an image of a conqueror-king whose true historical identity would become hopelessly entangled in a web of confusion designed to emphasize the magnificent liberation from the Babylonian Captivity.

Such is the origin of the story of the Babylonian king Nebuchadnezzar II (Akk Nabû-kudurri-usur, "Nabû protect my child") that would find its way into the books of the Old Testament. His name was identical to that of another Mesopotamian monarch, namely Nebuchadnezzar I of the second dynasty of Isin (1124-1103 B.C.).[2] It was he who, more than five centuries earlier, had defeated the forces of the kingdom of Elam in southwestern Iran during a period of turmoil after the collapse of the Kassite dynasty in Babylonia. Like his ancestor, Nebuchadnezzar II also appeared in a time of political upheaval after the fall of the Assyrian empire in 605 B.C. His father, Nabopolasar (626-605 B.C.), with the help of the Medes from northern Iran (see below, p. 17), had been largely responsible for both ending Assyrian domination and for founding the new Chaldean (or neo-Babylonian) kingdom in Mesopotamia. Unfortunately, Nabopolassar did not live long enough to realize his ultimate objective—the consolidation of his territorial gains and the complete rebuilding of the old capital of Babylon. His son, however, did.

As the second king of the Chaldean period (626-539 B.C.), Nebuchadnezzar II ruled for forty-three years (605-562 B.C.); his reign was the longest of any member of his dynasty. During that time, he organized massive building projects that were to transform his capital of Babylon into one of the seven wonders of the ancient world. He also led a number of military campaigns into Syria and Palestine that culminated in the conquest of Judah, the destruction of the temple of Solomon, and in the deportation of Hebrew captives into Babylonia. Thus it was he who began the infamous Babylonian Captivity prophesied by Jeremiah, a period of exile that lasted from 586 B.C. until Cyrus conquered Babylon. Given these achievements, it was only natural that, as was the case with Nebuchadnezzar I, his own contemporary cuneiform sources had to emphasize these successes, because both triumph in battle and the construction projects in Babylon would serve as symbols of the king's greatness to his own people. However, an accurate event-by-event account of what took place was not of primary importance; instead, he had to literally "glorify" his accomplishments. To understand why this was necessary, we must first consider the environmental and sociopolitical context in which the king lived before focusing our attention on the man Nebuchadnezzar II and the legends he inspired.

The Geographical Setting

The land known to the Greeks as Babylonia is synonymous with the southern portion of present-day Iraq. Extending roughly from Baghdad south to the Persian Gulf, it is characterized by rich alluvial soil deposited by the Tigris and Euphrates rivers as they flow south from their sources in the highlands of Asia Minor. Described by the historians of the second century B.C. as lower Mesopotamia (meaning "the land between the rivers"), Babylonia is quite dry, receiving less than four inches of precipitation annually. Hence, civilization as we know it could only exist when irrigation methods were developed and used. This irrigation was made possible by a phenomenon known as the annual flood. In early spring (March-April), the life-giving rivers began to rise, attaining their highest levels in June when they overflowed their banks in the lower reaches. Because the land was thus inundated when crops are normally grown, planting was done in the fall. Harvesting was completed during the following spring.

These hydrographic conditions could vary. Annual inundation was not always dependable, and lower than normal flood waters could combine with other factors and transform Babylonia into a land of turbulence. Although the Tigris-Euphrates valley, without irrigation, was generally inhospitable, no geographical barriers (including the Zagros mountains and the Syrian desert) existed to block numerous invasions of the area. Migration followed migration; reconquest followed conquest. Thus, while Egypt was largely isolated from the outside world, the history of Mesopotamia is quite different. The turbulence of invasion prevented the creation of a strong, unified nation. Such conditions inhibited the breakdown of localism and ensured instability from the time of the first appearance of urban centers to the fall of Babylon in 539 B.C.

Another significant factor contributing to the unsettled nature of Babylonia is that while essentially one ethnic group can be identified with Egyptian civilization and history, several play significant roles in the development of Mesopotamia. The first of these, the Sumerians, appeared around 3200 B.C. and introduced the art of writing to the Tigris-Euphrates valley. Their origins are unknown, but they lived in more or less independent city-states and were joined by Semites, who first appear in texts near Nippur in Babylonia and in northern Syria in the neighborhood of the recently excavated site of Ebla (Tell Mardikh) around 2600 B.C. It is quite possible, however, that these Semites arrived even earlier, because the date of the Ebla material is still hotly disputed. These people were family and tribally oriented and acquired many of the arts of civilization from the Sumerians, including writing, and preserved them for future peoples and generations. Among the earliest Semites were the Akkadians (ca. 2350 B.C.) and Amorites (ca. 2000 B.C.) who lived in Babylonia and who translated Sumerian texts and gave their gods semitic names. Later, in the middle of the second millennium B.C., another important group of these tribes, the Aramaeans, appeared on the scene. It was they who, over several centuries, conquered their neighbors and established the famous Assyrian empire.

The Chaldeans

By the time of Nebuchadnezzar, Babylonia had passed through nearly three millenia of conquest and city building; the "tradition" was to continue. His dynasty marks the creation of the neo-Babylonian empire that continued to flourish until the arrival of the Persians. It, too, illustrates just how complex things had become by 605 B.C. Nebuchadnezzar and his predecessors were Chaldeans, a term the Greeks used to denote particular tribes of *Kaldu* who eventually overthrew the powerful Assyrian empire and established their capital at Babylon.[3] Although we still don't know just how and when these people arrived in Mesopotamia, one fact is certain. The Chaldeans, like the Amorites and Akkadians before them, were family and tribally oriented, giving allegiance to individual sheikhs who might lead them in triumph against any foe, even Aramaeans. The *Kaldu* tribes already possessed the extreme southern part of Babylonia by the second half of the ninth century and had adopted the worship of the supreme god Marduk. Northward expansion put them in direct conflict with semitic Aramaean tribes collectively called *Aramu*.[4] Their supreme god was Sin, a god whose worship was centered at Ur in the south and Harran in the north. In 729 B.C., Tiglath-Pileser III, the Assyrian king who conquered Israel, ended the independence of Babylon. "In the northern Babylonian cities the priests and bureaucrats became the mainstay of Assyrian rule, and the initiative in the battle for independence passed into the hands of Chaldeans, who attracted the sympathy of the lower classes."[5] The later Assyrian king Sennacherib (705-681 B.C.) "came down like a wolf on the fold" and destroyed Babylon, which lay in ruins until his son and successor Esarhaddon (681-669 B.C.) ordered it rebuilt (by divine order, he maintained). The next two monarchs, Aššurbanipal and his brother, Šamaš-šum-ukin, partitioned the whole of Mesopotamia into two kingdoms, north and south, owing their allegiance to different sovereigns. But after a revolt in 652 B.C., Babylonia once again became part of the Assyrian empire, and it remained so for the next twenty-five years.

The Revolt of Nabopolassar

Finally, however, the immense size and internal weakness of Assyria took their toll. In Arahsamnu, 626 B.C., the *Kaldu* sheikh Nabopolassar, who also was the Assyrian governor of southern Babylonia, led an uprising and, on the twenty-sixth day of the month, declared himself "king of Babylon."[6] Called Belesys by the Hellenistic writers, Nabopolassar knew that his former overlord would not surrender territory easily. In fact, both he and the Assyrian king Aššur-etil-ilani (who was likely the predecessor of the *Sin-šarra-iškun* known to the Babylonians) claimed authority over Babylonia. Although the story of the struggle between these men for possession of southern Mesopotamia lies somewhat beyond the scope of this inquiry, it is clear from the account of the Babylonian priest Berossus (written in the third century B.C.) that war continued for several years:

> After him Sarakos reigned over the Assyrians. When he learned that a warrior people which had been formed from different bands was coming up from the sea to attack him, he quickly sent Bupolasaros to Babylon as general. But Bupolasaros, after deciding to rebel, arranged a marriage between Amhudin, the daughter of Astyages, the chief of the Medes, and his son Nabuchodrossoros. And swiftly setting out he moved to attack Ninos.[7]

It was only when Nabopolassar allied himself with the powerful Medes of northern Iran that the tide of battle began to turn. Originally a loosely organized group of Indo-European tribes, the Medes had been brought together through the efforts of a certain Huvakshatra, known to Herodotus and the later Greek writers as Cyaxeres. According to the classical account, he aided the Chaldeans in defeating Assyria:

> He is said to have been a much greater warrior than his father; it was he who first arrayed the men of Asia into companies and set each kind in bands apart, the spearmen and the archers and the horsemen; before this they were all blended alike confusedly together. This was the king who fought against the Lydians when the day was turned to night in the battle, and who united under his dominion all Asia that is beyond the river Halys. Collecting all his subjects, he marched against Ninus, wishing to avenge his father and to destroy the city. He defeated the Assyrians in battle.[8]

In the first century B.C. an account of the friendship between the Chaldeans and the Medes found its way into the *Universal History* of Diodorus Siculus. Although it roughly parallels the version of Herodotus quoted above, it suggests that such an alliance would be beneficial to both parties:

> A certain Arbaces, a Mede by race, and conspicuous for his bravery and nobility of spirit, was the general of the contingent of Medes which was sent each year to Ninus. And having made the acquaintance during this service of the general of the Babylonians, he was urged by him to overthrow the empire of the Assyrians. Now this man's name was Belesys, and he was the

most distinguished of those priests whom the Babylonians call Chaldeans.
And since as a consequence he had the fullest experience of astrology and
divination, he was wont to tell the future unerringly to the people in general;
therefore, being greatly admired for this gift, he also predicted to the
general of the Medes, who was his friend, that it was certainly fated for him
to be king over all the territory which was then held by Sardanapallus.
Arbaces, commending the man, promised to give him the satrapy of
Babylonia when the affair should be consummated, and for his part, like a
man elated by a message from some god, both entered into a league with the
commanders of the other nations and assiduously invited them all to
banquets and social gatherings, establishing thereby a friendship with each
of them. He was resolved also to see the king face to face and to observe
his whole manner of life.   Consequently he gave one of the eunuchs a
golden bowl as a present and gained admittance to Sardanapallus; and when
he had observed at close hand both his luxuriousness and his love of
effeminate pursuits and practices, he despised the king as worthy of no
consideration and was led all the more to cling to the hopes which had been
held out to him by the Chaldean. And the conclusion of the matter was that
he formed a conspiracy with Belesys, whereby he should himself move the
Medes and Persians to revolt while the latter should persuade the
Babylonians to join the undertaking and should secure the help of the
commander of the Arabs, who was his friend, for the attempt to secure the
supreme control.

When the year's time of their service in the king's army had passed and,
another force having arrived to replace them, the relieved men had been
dismissed as usual to their homes, thereupon Arbaces persuaded the Medes
to attack the Assyrian kingdom and the Persians to join in the conspiracy, on
the condition of receiving their freedom. Belesys too in similar fashion both
persuaded the Babylonians to strike for their freedom, and sending an
embassy to Arabia, won over the commander of the people of that country,
a friend of his who exchanged hospitality with him, to join in the attack.
And after a year's time all these leaders gathered a multitude of soldiers and
came with all their forces to Ninus, ostensibly bringing up replacements, as
was the custom, but in fact with the intention of destroying the empire of the
Assyrians.[9]

Whatever the reason, Nabopolassar and Cyaxeres united their forces
and prepared to engage the Assyrians and their Egyptian allies.
Pockets of resistance to the Chaldeans now developed in Babylonia (in
Uruk and Nippur), complicating an already confused situation.
Focusing on these important strongholds, the Assyrians tried to take

advantage of an apparent disunity and held out for almost seven years. Conditions became so deplorable that some Babylonians took to selling their own children into slavery to prevent them from starving to death.[10] By 615, Nippur had fallen into Nabopolassar's hands, freeing him to press his advantage into Assyria in an attempt to take Aššur and Nineveh. The Medes and their Scythian allies, however, actually took Aššur before the Chaldean host could arrive. There, Nabopolassar and Cyaxeres concluded a peace treaty, and two years later, in 612, Nineveh was taken. Although Cyaxeres now had an opportunity to share in the spoils of conquest alluded to in Diodorus Siculus's account, he instead retreated to his homeland.

In 609 B.C., the last king of the Assyrian empire, Aššur-uballit II, organized one final, futile attempt to recover lost territory. The northern city of Harran was to be the focal point of such efforts, but it eventually fell in a later year and the remaining troops retreated into Syria. The Egyptian monarch Necho II of the twenty-sixth (or Saite) dynasty feared both the Medes and the Chaldeans as much as had his predecessors. Furthermore, years earlier the Egyptians had become friends of the Assyrians, and the collapse of their empire would disastrously upset the balance of power in Mesopotamia and Syria. To avoid this, in 608, the pharaoh marched his armies across Palestine and reached the Euphrates River, where he spent the better part of three years fighting against Nabopolassar's forces in a lost cause.[11] While advancing eastward, Necho easily disposed of the forces of Josiah, the king of Judah, at Megiddo, when he foolishly attempted to block his path. In 605, the end for the Assyrians finally came at Carchemish.

The Rise of Nebuchadnezzar

Nabopolassar's original claim to kingship over Babylonia made twenty-five years earlier had been purely nominal. But by 605 B.C., the reverse was true. Nineveh lay in ruins; the Medes and Egyptians were no longer a threat to anyone, and southern Mesopotamian cities were dating their documents according to the appropriate year of the reign of Nabopolassar, "king of Babylon." Yet two decades of war meant that the king could hardly devote the time necessary to pressing affairs in the capital. Esarhaddon, it is true, had rebuilt the city; but it was not then the headquarters of an imperial administrative bureaucracy, nor was it the home of Aššur, the national god of the Assyrian empire. Now, however, with the independent Chaldean dynasty firmly in control, the supremacy of Marduk of Babylon, the "king of the gods" of the Babylonian Creation Epic, must once again become accepted fact. His temple, the Esagila, and the *ziqqurat* Etemenanki (the infamous tower of Babel of the Book of Genesis), had to be restored, and a fortification wall had to be built. Unfortunately, while all of this work still lay ahead, Nabopolassar died in his hour of triumph over Assyria. Having lived long enough to gain recognition of his kingship over Babylonia, his rule passed into the hands of his son, the crown-prince Nebuchadnezzar who, over the next forty-three years, amply justified the characterization of Megathenes and other classical writers by becoming a monarch whose achievements surpassed even those of his father.[12]

Nebuchadnezzar, like Alexander the Great of Macedonia, was hardly lacking in needed experience when he ascended the throne. In fact, he played a significant role in the battle of Carchemish and was in the process of pursuing the Egyptians on the way to final victory when he received news of his father's death. The Babylonian chronicler recorded the event in the following words:

(The twenty-first year): The king of Akkad stayed home (while) Nebuchadnezzar (II), his eldest son (and) crown prince, mustered (the army of Akkad). He took his army's lead and marched to Carchemish which is on the bank of the Euphrates. He crossed the river (to encounter the army of Egypt) which was encamped at Carchemish (. . .) They did battle together. The army of Egypt retreated before him. He inflicted a (defeat) upon them (and) finished them off completely.

In the district of Hamath the army of Akkad overtook the remainder of the army of (Egypt which) managed to escape (from) the defeat and which was not overcome. They (the army of Akkad) inflicted a defeat upon them (so that) a single (Egyptian) man (did not return) home. At that time Nebuchadnezzar (II) conquered all of Ha(ma)th.

For twenty-one years Nabopolassar ruled Babylon. On the eighth day of the month of Ab he died. In the month of Elul Nebuchadnezzar (II) returned to Babylon and on the first day of the month Elul he ascended the royal throne in Babylon.[13]

Once installed as a king, Nebuchadnezzar proceeded to fulfill the obligations expected of him, both in Babylon and elsewhere.

Folklore and the Written Source

The foregoing account of the rise of the Chaldean dynasty to prominence brings us to the reasons for the present investigation. Considering that Nabopolassar reigned only twenty-one years, we might expect even more information about his son's achievements. Remarkably, however, less is known from Mesopotamian sources of Nebuchadnezzar than about the reign of almost any other king of the Chaldean period. Although the last half century has yielded, among other things, an account of the war against Judah and the attempted siege of Jerusalem, the fact remains that information relating to both the destruction of the temple of Solomon in 586 B.C. (mentioned in the Old Testament) and other military campaigns the king may have conducted is almost totally lacking in Mesopotamian sources. Hence historians, for better or worse, are forced to probe the Hebrew, Latin, Greek, and Arabic secondary materials (as well as the dated cuneiform contract tablets) in the hope of determining what actually happened during this period. Obviously, there are hazards involved with such an investigation. Among other things, it brings into question the definition of history as opposed to tradition and might lead to doubts about the accuracy of these sources. Nevertheless, this approach seems worthwhile for two reasons. First, as already noted, most of the nonliterary documents are fragmentary and, as such, say little about the significant events of this age. Second, many of the Greek, Latin, Arabic, and Hebrew sources have yet to be utilized fully. Furthermore, stories about Nebuchadnezzar surviving from later antiquity appear to preserve peculiar folkloristic traditions and raise intriguing questions that have yet to be addressed fully. Why, for example, is Nebuchadnezzar so prominent in these later commentaries? What did the "historical" king accomplish that established his villainous reputation? Finally, what did Nebuchadnezzar *mean* to the various cultures that preserve mention of him in their sources? The answers to such questions would give us an opportunity to characterize both the individual being described and the "world views" that such characterizations represented.

It is with these questions in mind that the surviving accounts of Nebuchadnezzar's reign will be examined in the following chapters. Before proceeding, however, we must examine the role tradition or folklore played in the shaping of characterizations of Nebuchadnezzar. Unfortunately, however, determining the nature of folklore itself is a difficult task. There are as many definitions of folklore as there are elements to be considered.[14] In fact, many believe the term folklore is inadequate and does not really describe the cultural elements being discussed, especially because those who invented the term in the nineteenth century had a completely different notion of what the term meant.[15]   Certainly, oral transmission is an important aspect that is always associated with it; Bascom[16], Utley, and particularly Olrik[17] have stressed this factor in their analyses. Olrik even went so far as to suggest the existence of certain "epic laws" common to and governing the folk narrative as a whole, while at the same time indicating that these principles are applicable almost exclusively only to an oral tradition associated with *European* folklore. However, the term itself involves far more than just an emphasis on the oral element; as a result of the development of folkloristic approaches to the study of certain groups of people there has inevitably arisen the question of just who the "folk" actually are. Attempts at the identification of the folk began to surface as early as the nineteenth century, when it was common to associate this distinction with "the illiterate in a literate society."[18] This view has mostly been discarded[19], because the point has been made that literacy and improved technology are actually increasing the speed with which folklore is being transmitted.[20] The folk, in fact, are both the uneducated and the literate aristocracy responsible for the written transmission of folkloristic elements. This distinction applies to the people of the ancient Near East as well as to present-day civilizations.

Therefore, it would, be a mistake if we were to place emphasis on the oral aspect alone in the following discussion of source material[21]; as we have just seen, the written source can be just as significant a part of folklore as the oral and, in many cases, is more important. In the ancient Near East, the writings of the Hebrews constitute a case in point. Leaving aside the complicated, sometimes confusing arguments surrounding the date and authorship of the books of the Old Testament, there can be no question that the contents of several of them have true historical antecedents.   The present versions, however, may be embellished with folkloristic elements taken from stories that originally had entirely different functions; sources that may have been accurate in what they reported are transformed into descriptions that serve purely didactic purposes. The actual historical event thus becomes clouded within a mist of details that originally had no relationship to it. The point here is that, as Olrik himself asserts when speaking of "epic laws" which govern the *European* folk narrative, these so-called laws are not universal in any sense. Despite attempts to find similar modes of expression in the sources to be associated with several cultures, the lore of a particular folk, while appearing to have cross-cultural connections in the elements used in a particular characterization is, nevertheless, strikingly different in *structure* and *purpose*.

Characterizations that, on the surface, appear to be common in the lore
of all ancient cultures turn out to be not functionally similar at all.
Likewise, while oral transmission is certainly fundamental to it, the
disassociation of descriptions growing out of an original written source
from folklore is both unwarranted and unrealistic. As we shall see,
both the written and the oral play a part in characterizations contained
in the Hebrew (as well as the classical) sources, especially those
associated with Exilic or Post-Exilic periods.

Thus, regarding the following commentary, Barre Toelken's
operational hypothesis is certainly applicable:

Actually, *folklore* is a word very much like *culture*; it represents a
tremendous spectrum of human expression that can be studied in a number
of ways and for a number of reasons . . . The process of folklore may be
said in this sense to be local, communal, and informal. This does not argue
that formal people have no folklore, or that folklore will not be passed
among members of a highly trained profession. Rather, it suggests that even
in the most formal groupings of any society, active traditions are passed not
as a part of the formal training but as units of meaning interchanged
commonly enough with other familiar people that a recognizable clustering
of premises, formulas, and styles is built up and transmitted out of which
the informal performer acts.[22]

2

The Cuneiform Sources

"All of his toil he engraved on a stone stela"

— *Epic of Gilgamesh*, Tablet I

It should not be a surprise to see individuals in any culture desiring to preserve records of their achievements. Whether motivated by personal vanity, political necessity, or other concerns, human beings have for the better part of five millenia tried to give written accounts of themselves. Without written sources, the events of antiquity would today be largely a mystery, and cultures of the ancient Near East would be at the mercy of the archaeologist or "philosopher" to describe, at the very best, in an abstract or theoretical manner. Hence, before we examine what survives, a few comments on the nature of writing in Chaldean Mesopotamia are in order.

Cuneiform writing — wedges impressed with a reed stylus on a clay tablet — was invented in Mesopotamia to meet the needs of the bureaucratic state.[1] Scribal schools designed to teach the art of writing Sumerian (and later, Akkadian) cuneiform emerged in urban centers and continued to exist long after Sumerian and Akkadian ceased to be spoken languages. Early school exercise tablets show that particular texts could be copied over and over again, perhaps by several different individuals.[2] Through the training received in the *edubba* ("tablet house"), the scribe could "satisfy the economic and administrative needs of the land, primarily, of course, those of the temple and palace."[3] Although comparatively little has survived from the Old Babylonian period and early first millenium, documents from the seventh and sixth centuries indicate that scribal activity expanded in urban centers such as Uruk to include the preservation and copying of literary texts composed much earlier.[4] In addition to the preparation of receipts, or ledgers, for the daily business of the temple, medical texts, hymns, rituals, and astrological and birth omens were copied and preserved for the future.[5]

We actually have no contemporary evidence or the training of scribes in the sixth century, but there is no reason to suppose that it varied greatly from what it had been previously. From earlier evidence we know that, as with the learning of any language or script, memorization played a very important part. Lists of signs, along with their pronunciations, had to be copied and recopied until the student had mastered all of them.[6] This scribal training resulted early in the creation of reference tools such as "syllabaries" (signs with their pronunciation written out phonetically), bilingual Sumerian-Akkadian "vocabularies" (combinations of Sumerian word signs and their pronunciations together with their corresponding Akkadian meanings), topically arranged lists of Sumerian words with their Akkadian meanings, and grammatical texts that were intended to help Akkadian scribes learn Sumerian morphology. Thus, as A. L. Oppenheim has put it, "the traditional bilinguality of the Mesopotamian scribe was maintained by the training in which a great deal of Sumerian material was used."[7] Both the "literary" and "economic" documents reflect this tradition. Such circumstances naturally led to the specialization of scribes and to the preservation of several categories of material, although present evidence does not allow us to determine precisely the extent of this latter aspect of the scribes' activities.

In attempting to deal with the neo-Babylonian scribes, as with scribes in any other period, one problem stands out: almost nothing is known of their background, position in society, or possible political influence. Although the goddess Nisaba and the god Nabû were, at times, patrons of this profession, their precise relationship to the scribal craft is still unclear. Scribes were probably trained to deal with virtually every category of material—from omen texts to plant and stone lists. However, the occurrence in the Neo-Assyrian period of a *tupšar enuma Anu Enlil* (the scribe of the series *enuma Anu Enlil*), who dealt with materials of an astrological or astronomical nature,[8] is one indication that a certain degree of specialization existed. Another involves those designated as "city scribes," who were significant administrative officials in the ninth, eighth, and seventh centuries. In focusing more precisely on the neo-Babylonian source material, it is important to note that (except perhaps for the third dynasty of Ur) more documents survive from the neo-Babylonian period than from any other. A rich corpus of contract tablets and administrative records from Uruk and its great Eanna sanctuary provides us with a fascinating picture of the public and private life of numerous temple scribes and aids in reconstructing the careers of these individuals and their responsibilities.

Scribes in the neo-Babylonian period were one of two types: "the literary scribe who had to be specially trained and underwent thorough schooling, and the scribes who knew enough to write out business documents but did not have any literary background."[9] This appears to have been the case in the Old Babylonian period as well. Much more, of course, is known of the activities of the men who "controlled the writing down of all legal, epistolary, business, and administrative documents," because the corpus of material in which their names are mentioned is extremely large. Although there have been suggestions that scribes belonged to some type of "guild" or "association,"[10] the evidence is still inconclusive because the personal and "family" names included in the documents do not hint at the existence of such groups.

Because the reign of Nebuchadnezzar encompassed four full decades, it is not surprising to find that a virtual mountain of "royal inscriptions"[11] survives the age; these tell of numerous building activities or "archaeological work" completed during his reign. In these inscriptions we find the first projection of an image of Nebuchadnezzar, namely, the image Nebuchadnezzar himself sought to promote. This image is grounded to some extent in the historical reality of Nebuchadnezzar's deeds. A recent exhaustive analysis[12] of the epithets associated with Nebuchadnezzar that are found in these royal inscriptions reveals the traditional devotion of a Mesopotamian monarch to care of temples and to the restoration of sanctuaries that had fallen into disrepair. More than sixty such epithets occur in the inscriptions of Nebuchadnezzar. A similar number can be found in inscriptions surviving from the reign of the last king of the Chaldean dynasty, Nabonidus (Akk. Nabû-na'id, "May Nabû be praised").[13] It is with the sources for this king that we also must deal, because tradition associated several of his deeds with Nebuchadnezzar. Both Nebuchadnezzar's and Nabonidus's epithets range from the simple designation "strong king" (*šarru dannu*) to complicated phrases emphasizing devotion to his gods and to the upkeep of their temples.[14] If one uses the definition of folklore given previously by Olrik[15], then certainly one must search in the secondary commentaries composed long after the Chaldean dynasty ended for references to these activities and, consequently, for a partial explanation of the traditions that grew up around these monarchs. As we will soon see, this is exactly what is found in the later sources, particularly those written in Greek and Latin.

Aside from the building inscriptions, there are other texts that give us valuable information that subsequently became part of a folkloristic tradition. This body of material is, in many respects, much more difficult to handle. For example, BM 21946 represents a chronicle in the "Babylonian" sense,[16] because it mentions only the campaigns the king conducted in a given year and, therefore, constitutes a somewhat dry, event-by-event record of what the scribe considered to be the important occurrences of each year.[17]   Noticeably absent from this chronicle are the numerous epithets found in the building inscriptions. On the other hand, the Wadi-Brisa Inscription, detailing an expedition conducted by Nebuchadnezzar into Syria,[18] is quite different in that it also provides us with a beautiful description of the king's attitude toward his responsibilities and his god that, centuries later, found its way into the secondary literature of other peoples. The last section of this text reads as follows:

> I wrote an inscription mentioning my name, . . . I erected for posterity. May future [kings] re[spect the *monuments*], remember the praise of the gods (inscribed thereupon). [He who] respects . . . my royal name, who does not abrogate my *statutes* (and) not change my decrees, [his throne] shall be secure, his [li]fe last long, his dynasty shall continue (lit., renew itself)! Rain from the sky, [fl]ood [water] from (the interior of) the earth shall be given to him con[tinually] as a present! He himself shall rule peacefully and in abundance.

> O Marduk, my lord, so remember my deeds favorably as good [deeds], may (these) my good deeds be always before your mind (so that) my walking in Esagila and Ezida—which I love—may last to old age. May I remain always your legitimate governor (*šakanakku*), may I pull your yoke till (I am) sated with progeny, may my name be remembered in future (days) in a good sense, may my offspring rule forever over the black-headed.[19]

Two pieces[20] of pro-Persian propaganda provide a very negative image of Nabonidus. The so-called *Verse Account of Nabonidus* is a reflection on the reign of the king composed by the priests of Marduk in Esagila after the takeover of Babylon by Cyrus. It was composed to justify the end of the Chaldean dynasty and the rise of Persia to prominence. In it, Nabonidus is characterized in unprecedented form as a king who neglected Marduk and attempted the worship of a new god whom no one had ever seen in the land:

> [He had made the image of a deity] which nobody had (ever) seen in (this) country

> [He introduced it into the temple] he placed (it) upon a pedestal;

> [. . .] he called it by the name of Nanna,

> [it is adorned with a . . . of lapis] lazuli, crowned with a tiara,

> [. . .]its appearance is (that of) the eclipsed moon,

[. . . the gest]ure of its hand is like that of the god Lugal.ŠU.DU,

[. . .] its head of hair [rea]ches to the pedestal,

[. . .in fr]ont of it are [placed the Storm] (abûbu) Dragon and the Wild Bull.[21]

Subsequently, the king's famous journey to Tema is portrayed, with emphasis on the consequences rather than the causes of it, especially the termination of the celebration of the New Year's festival.[22]

He let (everything) go, entrusted kingship to him

And, himself, he started out for a long journey,

The (military) forces of Akkad marching with him;

He turned towards Tema (deep) in the west.

He started out the expedition on a path (leading) to a distant (region). When he arrived there,

He killed in battle the prince of Tema,

Slaughtered the flocks of those who dwell in the city (as well as) in the countryside,

And he, himself, took residence in [Te]ma,

the forces of Akkad [were also stationed] there.

****

(Yet) he (continues) to mix up the rites, he confuses the (hepatoscopic) oracles [. . . .].

To the most important ritual observances he makes (lit: orders) an end;

As to the (sacred) representations in Esagila—representations which Ea-Mummu (himself) had fashioned—

He looks at the representations and utters blasphemies.[23]

As we shall see, it was this very act that precipitated an important folkloristic tradition among the Jews released from captivity by Cyrus (538 B.C.), a tradition that became caught and confused in a web of hatred directed against Nebuchadnezzar, the author of the destruction of Jerusalem mentioned in the Second Book of Chronicles.[24]

Similar in tone to the *Verse Account* is the *Cyrus Cylinder*, a royal inscription extolling Cyrus and detailing the transfer of power from Nabonidus. Like the preceding account, the evil deeds of the last neo-Babylonian monarch are detailed, with emphasis on the positive elements in the Achaemenid conquest of Babylonia. However, the *Cyrus Cylinder* is straightforward, whereas the *Verse Account* is highly imaginative and focuses on supposed "heretical acts" of Nabonidus to cast Cyrus's image in a favorable light. Passages relative to our subject read as follows:

The chief of the gods (Marduk) was enraged by their complaints (and he left) their region. The gods who dwelt amongst them left their sanctuaries, angered that Nabonidus had brought them into Babylon.

But the god Marduk. . .took pity on the people of Sumer and Akkad who had become like corpses, he was appeased and had mercy. Carefully looking through all lands he sought an upright prince after his own heart. Taking him by the hand he pronounced his name: "Cyrus, king of Anshan." He designated him for rule over everything. At his feet he subdued the Qutu and all the Ummanmanda. The black-headed people which Marduk had allowed him to conquer he always administered in truth and justice. The god Marduk, the great lord, guardian of his people, looked with joy upon his good works and upright heart. He commanded him to march to his city Babylon.[25]

These Persian texts are very similar in what they say about Nabonidus.[26] Yet they completely ignore the much more favorable viewpoint current in Nabonidus's own inscriptions, which portrayed the monarch as a penitent, reverent ruler who had respect for the past.[27] It is probable that the Jews of the Post-Exilic period were acquainted with *both* traditions[28] and simply emphasized the hostile opinions of the Marduk priests because they were tailor-made for the didactic materials incorporated into the Book of Daniel when it was written in the Hellenistic period.

What emerges from these cuneiform texts is a positive characterization of Nebuchadnezzar. For Nabonidus, we have both the positive sources (from his and his mother's inscriptions) and the negative pro-Persian material. The chronicles are essentially neutral, except that the section related to Nabonidus and Tema reads like a silent indictment. Although these sources clearly have political overtones, they nevertheless relate to "heroic" or "villainic" images dictated by the cultural attitudes responsible for their creation. As Toelken noted, an individual's deeds could be used by contemporary cultures to fit totally different paradigms for obviously instructional purposes.

3

The Classical, Medieval, and Hebrew Sources

Obviously, Nebuchadnezzar's own cuneiform sources leave much unsaid. Not only is the *Babylonian Chronicle* incomplete, but the many extant building inscriptions say little or nothing about important events. However, numerous Greek, Latin, and Hebrew secondary sources survive that reflect on Nebuchadnezzar's reign. They deal with the neo-Babylonian period as a whole, but they occasionally contain information regarding Nebuchadnezzar and Nabonidus not mentioned elsewhere. Several of these commentaries, unfortunately, are fragmentary, which makes the task of determining just how, when, and from whom information was transmitted very difficult. The discussion that follows, therefore, must of necessity be very technical. Some problems concerning the oral and/or written transmission of information are addressed, and a number of conclusions are offered. What I hope will result from this examination is an understanding of what Nebuchadnezzar and the Chaldeans meant to the historians or chroniclers of later antiquity and the Middle Ages.

The Greek Sources

Megasthenes, the earliest of the classical writers to mention Nebuchadnezzar, flourished at the time of Seleucus I Nicator (312-280 B.C.)[1]. An Ionian who wrote primarily on the geography and people of India, he participated in several embassies to that country between 302-291 B.C. dispatched to the court of the Indian king Sandrocottus.[2] His *History of India*, as Josephus tells us,[3] included in its fourth book a discussion of the Babylonian kings of the sixth century B.C., with particular attention paid to Nebuchadnezzar. Only a fragment of his work has survived, but it includes a dynastic list and has fortunately been preserved by a certain Abydenus (whose work will be discussed later) and this was in turn preserved by Eusebius. It reads in part as follows:

> Abydenus, in his history of the Assyrians, has preserved the following fragment of Megasthenes, who says: That Nabucodrosorus (Nebuchadnezzar), having become more powerful than Hercules, invaded Libya and Iberia, (Spain), and when he had rendered them tributary, he extended his conquests over the inhabitants of the shores upon the right of the sea. . .he expired, and was succeeded by his son Evilmarchus (Evil Merodach), who was slain by his kinsman, Neriglisares (Neriglissor), and Neriglisares left a son, Labassoarascus (Labarosoarchod), and when he also had suffered death by violence, they made Nabannidochus king, being of no relation to the royal race.[4]

We cannot, of course, determine exactly what sources Megasthenes used in the writing of this account. The lengths of the reigns of the kings are not designated in numbers of years, even though the list is correct. However, Megasthenes may have had access to cuneiform documents that were still being composed in the Hellenistic period and could read the script himself or had someone available who could read it for him. The relationship of one king to another in his list, in addition to his mention that Nabonidus was not related to any of his predecessors, seem to confirm this assertion.

Included in the fragment of Megasthenes is the story of Nebuchadnezzar relating to the last days of the Chaldean dynasty.

> It is, moreover, related by the Chaldeans, that as he went up into his palace he was possessed by some god; and he cried out, and said: "Oh! Babylonians, I, Nabucodrosorus (Nebuchadnezzar) foretell unto you a calamity which must shortly come to pass, which neither Belus my ancestor, nor his queen Beltis, have the power to persuade the Fates to turn away. A Persian mule shall come, and by the assistance of your gods shall impose upon you the yoke of slavery; the author of which shall be a Mede, the foolish pride of Assyria. Before he should thus betray my subjects, Oh! that some sea, or whirlpool, might receive him, and his memory be blotted out forever; or that he might be cast out to wander through some desert, where there are neither cities nor the trace of men; a solitary exile among rocks and caverns, where beasts and birds alone abide. But for me, before he shall have conceived these mischiefs in his mind, a happier end will be provided.[5]

This account cannot be found in any other source, although the equation of Nabonidus with the Mede Astyages appearing in the writings of Gerogius Syncellus suggests that this story (or something similar to it) was known much later and extracted from another source. The prophecy of Nebuchadnezzar raises a question quite germaine to our whole discussion, namely, the relationship of what has been called "apocalyptic literature" to an understanding of folklore.[6]   Herodotus frequently uses the phrase "the Chaldeans say" when describing features of the city of Babylon and thus gives the impression of his having incorporated information into his *Histories* which he obtained by word of mouth from the Babylonians themselves. Megasthenes, a Greek native of the Seleucid kingdom, does likewise here. However, while the form of this account conveys the impression of an orally transmitted tale, possibly reflecting a local oral tradition that existed contemporaneously with the written sources, recent research reveals that prophetic literature such as this constitutes a genre in itself and not only had a long written tradition but also was associated with the very Chaldean dynasty that Megasthenes is discussing.   The so-called *Dynastic Prophecy*[7] relating to the end days of the Chaldean era provides us with an Akkadian version that very closely parallels the Megasthenes fragment. When describing the reign of Nabonidus and the capture of Babylon by Cyrus, it relates the following information:

A re[bel] prince will arise [. . .]

The dynasty of Harran [he will establish.]

For seventeen years [he will exercise sovereignty].

He will oppress (lit. 'be stronger than') the land and the festival of Esa [gil he will cancel].

A fortress in Babylon [he will build].

He will plot evil against Akkad.

A king of Elam will arise, the scepter. . .[. . .]

He will remove him from his throne and [. . .]

He will take the throne and the king who arose from the throne [. . .]

The king of Elam will change his place [. . .]

He will settle him in another land [. . .][8]

This segment of the *Dynastic Prophecy* suggests that references in the writings of Megasthenes and Herodotus to Chaldeans and other people indicate written rather than oral transmission. The classical authors used documents composed by Chaldean scribes rather than relying on the "man on the street,"[9] and the method of relating the information contained in their accounts only leads to the formation of a faulty impression of oral transmission of details. The discovery of the *Dynastic Prophecy* makes it likely, as was the case with the *Prayer of Nabonidus*, that Megasthenes' account is rooted in a written tradition that was already well established when he incorporated it into his *History of India*. Olrik[10] insisted on disassociating anything "folkloristic" with transmission from an original written source. If that were true, then it would seem hard (on the surface, at least) to find folklore or popular tradition here, even though there is certainly nothing to prevent the oral transmission of such accounts from one generation to another. However, as we have seen already, written materials can have as much to do with folklore as the oral, and certainly seem to have formed an integral part of it in the Seleucid Near East.

Following closely after Megasthenes is Berossus, a Babylonian priest of the third century B.C., who wrote in Greek on Babylonian history. He was, as Josephus remarks, "a Chaldean by birth, but familiar in learned circles through his publication for Greek readers of works on Chaldean astronomy and philosophy." Josephus also says that Berossus followed "the most ancient records"[11] in the preparation of his history, known either as *Chaldaika* or *Babyloniaca*; his work was "dedicated to Antiochus Seleucus I (281-260 B.C.); apparently it was composed to provide the Macedonian king with the history of the land he ruled."[12] Like the history of Megasthenes, Berossus's *Babyloniaca* has perished, except for an important fragment that has been preserved both by Josephus and Eusebius.

Nabuchodonosor, after he had begun to build the above mentioned wall, fell sick, and departed this life, when he had reigned forty-three years; whereupon his son Evilmerodachus obtained the kingdom. He governed public affairs in an illegal and improper manner; and, by means of a plot laid against him by Neriglissoorus, his sister's husband, he was slain when he had reigned only two years. After his death, Neriglissor, who had conspired against him, succeeded him in the kingdom, and reigned four years. His son Laborosoarchodus, obtained the kingdom, although a mere child, and reigned nine months. But, on account of the evil practices which he manifested, a plot being made against him by his friends, he was tortured to death.

After his death, the conspirators having assembled, by common consent, put the crown on the head of Nabonnedus, a man of Babylon, one of the leaders of that insurrection . . . .In the seventeenth year of his reign, Cyrus came out of Persia.[13]

Of all the lists of neo-Babylonian monarchs that have survived, the arrangement of Berossus most closely corresponds to that of the cuneiform documents.[14]   Only in one instance, that of Labashi-Marduk, is there any discrepancy.   Obviously, if Berossus himself could not read the cuneiform script, at least someone must have been at hand who could read it for him.   As for Labashi-Marduk, it is unlikely (in view of his overall accuracy) that Berossus could have been incorrect in dating the reign of this latter monarch.   Why then (at least according to the dated economic texts) do the reigns of Labashi Marduk and his successor Nabonidus overlap by almost one month, and why are cuneiform tablets known which document only about two months of his reign?   It is possible that errors arising from manuscript transmission could have resulted in the nine-month figure given by Josephus.   This theory prompted Parker and Dubberstein to propose a plausible alternative hypothesis (i.e., that the Greek ø could have been mistaken for a ß).[15]   This seems all the more sensible, because the earliest text from the reign of Nabonidus (25 May 556 B.C.) is clearly dated nearly a full month before the latest document bearing the name of Labashi-Marduk (20 June 556 B.C.).

This list contains an interesting piece of information regarding Amel-Marduk and his successor Neriglissar that is not mentioned in any other source — that Neriglissar was the brother-in-law of Amel-Marduk. Thus far, no cuneiform evidence has been uncovered to lend support to this assertion, and no other writer before or after his time mentions it, though it is vaguely hinted at in Megasthenes.[16]

Alexander Polyhistor, our next source, was probably born about 105 B.C. in Miletus or Caria.   He was carried off as a prisoner of war to Rome during an age when feuds between Marian and Sullan factions were all too prevalent.   It is said that he was once the pedagogue of a certain Cornelius Lentulus and that he taught C. Julius Hyginus.   He received the name Polyhistor because of his "voluminous historical writings," which covered a number of countries and peoples, including the Jews.[17]   It seems that his works contained mostly material borrowed from other sources that no longer exist.[18]   Like

Megasthenes' *History of India*, Polyhistor's works have perished, but, again as with Megasthenes, portions are preserved in Eusebius. Included in these fragments is the following dynastic list:

> Then Nabupalsar (Nabopollassar), reigned 20 years; and after him Nabuchodrossorus (Nebuchadnezzar), reigned 43 years. . .And after Nabuchodrossorus his son, Amilmarudochus (Evil Merodach), reigned 12 years.

> And after him, Neglisarus (Neriglissor), reigned over the Chaldeans four years; and then Nabodenus (Nabonidus) reigned 17 years.[19]

The list is interesting for two reasons. First, Labashi-Marduk is omitted, for what reason we do not know. Second, and more important, figures given in all cases are correct except for the assignment of twelve years to Amel-Marduk. There does not seem to be any reason to dispute Olmstead's conclusion that Alexander Polyhistor "borrowed from Berossus direct,"[20] but why, then, are we presented with a twelve year reign for Amel-Marduk? Two explanations seem plausible. Either the manuscript of Polyhistor that Eusebius used (or some previous one, of which his was a copy) registered an *iota* (i) or (<) before the *beta* (ß) (assuming that numerical values were contained in it), or Eusebius himself was guilty of misreading the text.

The Hellenistic Age produced yet another writer whose work contains information regarding Nebuchadnezzar that is not to be found in any extant source. He is Eupolemus, a hellenized Jew of the second century B.C. who authored *On the Kings of Judaea* which, in its original form, may have begun with Adam and continued down to his own time.[21] What survives of his account of Nebuchadnezzar's siege of Jerusalem is extremely important, because it evinces a knowledge both of Jewish heritage and a decidedly cosmopolitan view of the history that resulted from the spread of Greek ideas to the east in the time of Alexander the Great.[22] In preparing his work, Eupolemus drew from materials contained in 2 Kings 24:12-13 and 25:13-17 as well as from sources probably written in Greek (i.e., Hecataeus and Ctesias, as well as the *Apocrypha*) that have long since disappeared.[23] His approach appears to be somewhat Herodotean, although it also contains earmarks of the "apocalyptic" element that is found in cuneiform texts from the Seleucid kingdom that are now undergoing considerable review.

Fragment Four of Eupolemus's *On the Kings of Judaea* contains, among other things, a long discussion of the Temple of Solomon and several brief references to Nebuchadnezzar's conquest of Jerusalem.[24] In the process, he associates the Medes with the Babylonian king and gives evidence of having woven accounts of Ctesias and Herodotus into an elaborate description that reflects attitudes seemingly prevalent in his own day. As Wacholder aptly puts it, "Eupolemus, it would seem, was comparing the political situation during the last years of the monarchy with that of his own time, when there was a close link between the Seleucid overlords and the Jewish Hellenizers. In both instances, a great power is said to have intervened on behalf of those who wished to reform the religious structure of the state. Babylon, like Assyria in former times, was the rod of Yahweh's anger."[25] As a result, Eupolemus creates an account that combines devices characteristic of Greek historiography with elements of the Babylonian apocalyptic. The description of Nebuchadnezzar appears to have had a *political* purpose that would have been recognized by the Jews of his own day. Like Megasthenes' writings, even the very brief surviving sections of *On the Kings of Judaea* appear to reflect a long written tradition at one time evident in the Seleucid cuneiform material that formed an important part of the "lore" of the Babylonians. This tradition subsequently found its way into a cosmopolitan Greek historiography; there it became divorced from the actual event (just as the Seleucid apocalyptic materials were in part) to serve purposes of a somewhat didactic nature.[26]

Another writer who has left us varied information concerning the neo-Babylonian period and particularly Nebuchadnezzar is Josephus, a Jewish general and historian of the first century A.D. He went to Rome during the reign of Vespasian, and later became a friend of the emperor's son Titus, in whose company he made a second trip to Rome after the fall of Jerusalem (A.D. 70).[27] In addition to his *Autobiography* and the *Jewish War*, he composed the *Contra Apionem* and the *Jewish Antiquities*, which cover the conquest of the Jews and the fall of Jerusalem in the time of Nebuchadnezzar as well as the release of Jehoiachin in the accession year of Amel-Marduk.

The information contained in his *Contra Apionem*, largely derived from Berossus,[28] requires no further comments. However, the *Jewish Antiquities* presents a multitude of problems that are not so easily solved. Some of what Josephus included concerning the Jew Jehoiachin, Amel-Marduk, and the other members of the eleventh Babylonian dynasty is not found in any other source. Furthermore, because of the varied character of this information, it is almost impossible to attribute the discrepancies to difficulties encountered through transmission of manuscript. To begin with, Josephus (like all the writers we have dealt with thus far) preserves a neo-Babylonian king list, which is totally unlike any we have heretofore encountered. After stating that Nebuchadnezzar lived "twenty-five years after the overthrow of Jerusalem," he continues as follows:

> After the death of Nebuchadnezzar his son Abilmathodochus, who took over the royal power, at once released Jechonias, the king of Jerusalem, from his chains and kept him as one of his closest friends, giving him many gifts and setting him above the kings in Babylonia. For his father had not kept faith with Jechonias when he voluntarily surrendered himself with his wives and children and all his relatives for the sake of his native city, that it might not be taken by siege and razed, as we have said before. When Abilmathadochus died after reigning eighteen years, his son Eglisaros took over the royal power and held it for forty years until the end of his life. After him the succession to the throne fell to his son Labosordachos and, after holding it nine months in all he died.[29]

Josephus continued on to say that Babylon was taken by Cyrus after Labashi-Marduk's successor, Nabonidus, who was also called Belshazzar, had reigned eighteen years.

The source of the information contained in Josephus's first statement concerning the release of Jehoiachin is clearly taken from 2 Kings 25:27-30 and Jeremiah 52:31-2 in which almost the exact same words occur. But what about the king list and the statement that Neriglissar was the son of Amel-Marduk? With the exception of the *Chronicle* of the Venerable Bede (who says he borrowed his material from the *Jewish Antiquities*), this list occurs nowhere else.[30] Josephus states several times that he never supplemented material from the Scripture with information gathered from other places,[31] yet here is clearly an instance where that has been done. "In not a few instances Josephus diverges from the text of Scripture, either from ignorance of Hebrew or of set purpose." It has been suggested that this divergence was "either due to a rationalistic endeavour to remove supposed difficulties, or else to ignorance or mistakes on his part."[32] However, there may be yet another reason for these chronological inconsistencies.

Unfortunately, as Feldman has pointed out,[33] few people have attempted to determine the sources Josephus used in the compilation of his *Jewish Antiquities*. Nevertheless, one or two conclusions can be drawn. First, Josephus probably obtained his nine-month figure for the reign of Labashi-Marduk from Berossus's *Babyloniaca* (from his list preserved in the *Contra Apionem*).   Second, the only sources containing any information that even approximates what is in the rest of the list are rabbinical works (to be discussed more fully later), composed long after Josephus wrote, and the *Book of Baruch* forming part of the *Apocrypha*.   The *Talmud* states that Nebuchadnezzar reigned forty-five years.[34]   However, both the *Talmud* and the midrashim forming what is known as the *Midrash Rabbah*[35] declare that Belshazzar was the successor of Amel-Marduk (perhaps because of the similarity of the names Bel-šarra-usur and Nergal-šarra-usur), leaving completely out of sequence Labashi-Marduk and (more importantly) Neriglissar, who is not mentioned in the midrashim or in the *Apocrypha* and who is given a forty-year reign in the *Jewish Antiquities*.   Also, the *Book of Baruch* fails to mention Amel-Marduk, but instead declares Belshazzar to be the successor of Nebuchadnezzar (as does Dan. 5).   Indeed, Amel-Marduk is not even mentioned in the *Apocrypha*.[36]   Furthermore, the *Talmud* assigns a twenty-three year reign to Amel-Marduk (based, it is said, on Jewish tradition), a figure that has no previous parallel elsewhere, including the works of Josephus.   Finally, Josephus's comment that Nabonidus and Belshazzar are one and the same person cannot be found in any source (except Bede's *Chronicle*).   Because the author of the *Jewish Antiquities* was well acquainted with Berossus, and because neither his figures nor relationships are in accord with even existing rabbinical works, several analysts, Smith and Wace included, have assumed that Josephus was either possessed of a superficial knowledge of Jewish tradition, or he altered it inexplicably.[37]   However, his obvious unwillingness to tamper with the account given in the Old Testament points either in the direction of still another source used by Josephus that is no longer extant or to an oral tradition that was far removed from the period being described and therefore unreliable.

The second century A.D. produced another writer, noted for his versatility and meticulousness, whose work contains mention of our period.   This is Claudius Ptolemy, whose studies in the field of geography, astronomy, and mathematics are well known to the student of ancient history.   His famous *Ptolemaic Canon* preserves (with one exception) in order the names of the Chaldean monarchs from Nabopolassar through Nabonidus and includes the lengths of their reigns.

Although the list is correct in the number of regnal years, it does not mention Labashi-Marduk.[38]   Such also was the case with Polyhistor's list, as we have seen.[39]   But did Ptolemy leave him out of the list because he used Polyhistor (who depended on Berossus) as a source, or because he thought him too insignificant to include in his canon?   The second conclusion is certainly possible, because a discrepancy exists between Polyhistor and the *Ptolemaic Canon* in the number of years assigned to Amel-Marduk, although this may be the result of an error on the part of Eusebius. We will never know, of course, but if he derived his information directly from Berossus, one wonders why his list is incomplete.

The last of the writers normally included in this group requires little explanation. This is Abydenus, whom we have already encountered. Writing in the second or third century A.D., he was largely a preserver of information contained in the older works composed before his time. His great work, *About the Assyrians*, included segments from Alexander Polyhistor and Megasthenes. The work has perished, but, thanks to Eusebius, the fragment of Megasthenes that he included in his book dealing with the neo-Babylonian period has survived.[40]

Late Roman and Medieval Sources

The third and fourth centuries of the Christian era witnessed the production of numerous chronicles that were intended to be records of important historical events from the time of Adam to their composition. Perhaps the most famous of these was the *Chronicle* of Eusebius Pamphilius, or Eusebius, Bishop of Caesarea (ca. A.D. 265-340). The *Chronicle* commenced with the birth of Abraham and terminated (until Jerome extended it during the course of translating it into Latin) in A.D 342. Eusebius used the previous work of Julius Africanus as a model, and the result was "a comparative chronology of all known people." The finished product "was, above all, apologetic, the author wishing to prove by means of it that the Jewish religion, of which the Christian was the legitimate continuation, was older than the oldest of heathen cults, and thus deprive pagan opponents of their taunt of novelty, so commonly hurled against Christianity."[41] It was divided into two books, with the first continuing in narrative form to A.D. 329, and the second consisting of chronological tables (Olympiads, consular *fasti*, Egyptian, Assyrian and Babylonian king lists, and so on). In all cases Eusebius considered Jewish history as "the point of departure of all peoples. Every date in the end is calculated according to the chronology of the Bible, even the succession of Roman emperors."[42] The Greek version of the text is lost, but Greek fragments survive, as well as Armenian, Syriac, and Latin (Jerome) translations.

The importance of the *Chronicle* lies not in the fact that it sheds new light on Nebuchadnezzar's reign or the reign of any neo-Babylonian monarch, for there is nothing in it (except one short comment in

Book 3)[43] that is not found elsewhere. It is noteworthy because it preserves not only Berossus (through Josephus) but also those fragments of Megasthenes (via Abydenus) and Polyhistor that otherwise would have been totally lost to us.

Eusebius Sophonius Hieronymus, more often referred to as St. Jerome (A.D. 340-420) is yet another writer who dealt with Mesopotamian and Jewish history in the sixth century B.C. Although he is better known for his Latin Vulgate Bible and his translation of Eusebius' *Chronicle*, he also was responsible for composing commentaries on several books of the Old Testament, including Daniel and Isaiah. These are important for our purposes, because some of the information he includes is not found in any source, including the rabbinical works.

First, his *Commentary on Daniel*, chapter 5:1, includes a king list, commencing with Nebuchadnezzar and ending with Belshazzar.[44] His list is an unbroken succession from father to son. What is interesting is that Nebuchadnezzar is the only king to whom a definite number of years is assigned. Also, Belshazzar is mentioned as having been the son of Labshi-Marduk; this cannot be found in any other source. Jerome himself says that he got his information from Josephus (his exact words are *refert indem Iospehus*), probably from his *Jewish Antiquities*, Book 10, 11, 2. Yet Jerome does not mention the lengths of the reigns of the kings, nor does he equate the name Nabonidus with Belshazzar, as we have seen Josephus do. Because there is no mention in the *Jewish Antiquities* of the relationship of Labashi-Marduk to Belshazzar, perhaps Jerome simply implied what he thought was obvious.

Further information regarding Amel-Marduk lies specifically in Jerome's *Commentary on Isaiah*. It concerns his accession to the throne after Nebuchadnezzar's death. According to this source, the "magnates of the state" objected to his ascending to the throne because they feared Nebuchadnezzar might somehow return. Hence, they prevented him from doing so. Jerome describes this incident as "a fable told by the Hebrews" (*narrant Hebraei huius modi fabulam*).[45] Yet this fable is not found in any rabbinical source, nor is it mentioned elsewhere.

The *Liber Genealogus* or *Liber Generationis*, like the several chronicles before it, deals with Jewish and Mesopotamian history in the time of Nebuchadnezzar. Composed probably in the fifth century of the Christian era,[46] this work included the earlier composition of Hippolytus of Porta, a contemporary of Clement of Alexandria and Tertullian (which in turn was based on that of Julius Africanus), and it probably served as a source for the later *Chronicle of Fredegar*.[47] In mentioning Amel-Marduk (called Ulemadar) and the release of the Jew Jehoiachin (Iechonias) it gives no new information, but merely reiterates what is contained in the Bible (Jeremiah 52:31-3 and 2 Kings 25:27-30) and in Josephus (*Jewish Antiquities* 10. 11 2).[48]

The seventh, eighth, and ninth centuries produced three additional chroniclers in whose works references to Nebuchadnezzar occur. The first of these, the Venerable Bede (672-735), probably composed his *Chronicle* around A.D. 730. In it he utilized not only the Old Testament (Jer. and 2 Chron.) and the writings of St. Augustine and Ambrose, but also those of Eusebius, Jerome (his *Commentary on Daniel* is often quoted), and especially Josephus.[49] In fact, it is from the tenth book of the *Jewish Antiquities* that his neo-Babylonian list comes. Furthermore, his stories of the beginning of the Captivity and the final release of Jehoiachin are drawn directly from the Book of Jeremiah.[50]

On the surface at least, Bede poses the fewest problems for the historian. His sources seem easy to determine, at least in this instance. However, for years medievalists have focused their attention on his numerous references to Josephus. Did he actually have a copy of the *Jewish Antiquities* in his library, or did he use an intermediate source? If he depended on another author's work, what was it? This question prompted the following comment from M. L. W. Laistner:

Bede's acquaintance with the writings of Josephus is a matter of considerable complexity . . . it is not clear whether Bede was using a Latin translation of the *Antiquities* or an intermediate source, or the Greek original . . . But, indeed, appeals to the authority of Josephus are exceedingly numerous in our quarter, particularly in the commentaries devoted to the historical books of the Old Testament. Some of Bede's citations or adoptions from Josephus were made directly from that historian, while others were taken over from Rufinus or perhaps Jerome. But whether Bede read Josephus in the original Greek must remain undecided still.[51]

In spite of Laistner's comments, the evidence strongly suggests that Bede drew his information from the *Jewish Antiquities*. It is certainly possible that Bede derived his neo-Babylonian royal list and the details concerning Amel-Marduk's release of Jehoiachin from an intermediate source. However, as has already been noted, the list that Bede preserves exists in no other source except Book 10 of the *Jewish Antiquities*. Although it is true that Jerome's list was probably based on the same material, his account is far from being the exact duplicate of Josephus that Bede's is. The question of Bede's sources, of course, will never be resolved to everyone's satisfaction. Yet, in view of what his *Chronicle* contains with reference to our period, he probably possessed a copy (either in Greek or Latin) of Josephus's *Jewish Antiquities*, from which he cited directly.

The so-called *Chronicon Paschale* of the seventh century A.D.,[52] like Bede's *Chronicle*, preserves the names of the Chaldean kings, especially those of Nebuchadnezzar and Amel-Marduk. Also published under the titles *Fasti Siculi, Chronicon Alexandrinum*, and *Chronicon Constantinopolitanum*,[53] this work constitutes a record of important historical events from the time of Adam to A.D 629. Its organizer was a clerical contemporary of the Byzantine monarch Heraclius (610-41)[54] who completed the work sometime between A.D 630 and 640. In its finished form it thus constituted an extension of the previous chronicles of Julius Africanus and Eusebius (which probably served as two of its sources).[55]

Nebuchadnezzar, Amel-Marduk, Jehoiachin, and Belshazzar are mentioned in two places in the *Chronicon Paschale*. In neither case is it difficult to determine the source of the composer's information.[56] The first account is a verbatim reproduction of Jeremiah 52:31 and 2 Kings 25:27 of the Old Testament and Josephus's *Jewish Antiquities* 10. 11 2.[57] The second is a verbatim copy as well (in which it is stated that Amel-Marduk was the brother of Belshazzar),[58] only this time taken directly from Book 2 of Eusebius's *Chronicle*, the only other place in which it appears.

Georgius Syncellus, the last of the medieval sources, was a Byzantine chronicler of the late eighth and early ninth centuries. As his name implies, he was the "confident companion" of the patriarch of Constantinople and from 784-806 was in the service of Tarausius.[59] On his retirement, he completed his *Chronographia*, which included events from Adam to Diocletian. Syncellus is extremely important, because he not only preserves information contained in Eusebius's *Chronicle*, but also includes segments of the *Ptolemaic Canon* and Josephus.

To say that Syncellus poses problems is an understatement. His *Chronographia* has king lists everywhere, and each one is different from the one that precedes or follows it. He had so many sources with which to deal that his attempt to give "equal time" to all resulted in total confusion. To begin with, Syncellus's version of the *Ptolemaic Canon*[60] provides information regarding the period of Nabopolassar through Nabonidus. One notices striking differences between his account[61] and the section of the *Ptolemaic Canon* cited previously.[62] Although both sources leave Labshi-Marduk out of the list, the years assigned to Amel-Marduk, Neriglissar, and Nabonidus by Syncellus are strikingly different from those cited before. In addition, Nabonidus is equated with Astyages. This does not occur in any source, although it is reminiscent of Josephus's relating Nabonidus to Belshazzar.

To complicate matters further, a second king list is included, which Syncellus states is derived from "ecclesiastical computation." The section relevant to our period is the total antithesis of the one cited previously. Not only are the figures for Amel-Marduk and Neriglissar reversed, but now for the first time Neriglissar is equated with Belshazzar and Astyages, Darius, Xerxes, and Artaxerxes are all declared to be one and the same person—namely Nabonidus — who is said to have ruled seventeen years. This list is repeated elsewhere in his *Chronographia*,[63] as is the fragment of Berossus quoted in Josephus's *Contra Apionem*.

The confusion of both names and years found in the *Chronographia* is probably the result of Syncellus's own carelessness. His work mentions every Greek source, from Megasthenes to Claudius Ptolemy, but he probably knew most of them only through Eusebius's *Chronicle*. He may have had copies of Josephus's *Contra Apionem* (in which Berossus's chronology is preserved) and the *Jewish Antiquities*,[64] as well as the Scriptures. His attempt to incorporate all of this material into his work, however, resulted in erroneous quotations and misattributions.[65] Although part of the fault certainly lies in the manuscripts he used, much is contained in the *Chronographia* that cannot be dismissed on these grounds alone. His own carelessness seems a more likely cause of these discrepancies.

Finally, the end of the fifteenth century witnessed the publication of the so-called *Antiquitatum Variarum Volumina* XVII. It first appeared in Venice in 1498 and was commented on by the "notorious monk" Annius Viterbensis. Its importance for our purposes is that it includes a neo-Babylonian king list supposedly lifted from the writings of Megasthenes. However, as J. W. Bosanquet pointed out long ago, "it has been copied unfortunately by some illiterate interpreter of history, who has largely interpolated his own imperfect ideas concerning the Babylonian kings, and owing to these interpolations, the passage has generally been rejected as spurious and worthless."[66] The list reads as follows:

Nabugodonosor, annis 45;
Amilinus Evilmerodach, annis 30;
Filius hujus primus Ragassar, annis 3;
Secundus Lab-Assardoch, annis 6;

Tertius Baltassar, annis 5.[67]

When compared to the fragment of Megasthenes (preserved by Eusebius though Abydenus) previously cited,[68] one immediately notices a number of striking differences. First, although no numerical figures appear in the preceding list, the *Antiquitatum Variarum Volumina* XVII asserts nevertheless that Neriglissar, Labashi-Marduk, and Belshazzar were all sons of Amel-Marduk. Second, the numbers of years given are not in accord with any list, not even those contained in Syncellus's *Chronographia*. What source (or sources) did the author use? Probably the Hebrew works, namely the *Talmud* and the *Chronicle* of Jerachmeel.[69] The figure of forty-five years assigned to Nebuchadnezzar is found only in the *Talmud*, while the assertion that Amel-Marduk's three "successors" were all his sons has no parallel except in the Hebrew *Chronicle* of Jerachmeel. Annius therefore must have been acquainted with the *Talmud* and falsely attributed information taken from these works to Megasthenes.

The Hebrew Sources

The rabbinical works and Hebrew chronicles contain a wealth of interesting and unusual information regarding Nebuchadnezzar that is not found in any other source. Of course, most of it can be dismissed as mere Jewish folklore; nevertheless, as such it is well suited to the purposes of this investigation. When compared to the writings of Josephus and the books of Jeremiah, 2 Kings, and 2 Chronicles of the Old Testament, some peculiar similarities and contrasts can be distinguished, which makes an examination of their contents all the more worthwhile.

Apart from the Old Testament, perhaps the earliest of these works is the *Talmud*. The word, meaning teaching, actually refers to two different products, one of the Palestinian (*Jerusalem Talmud*) and one of the Babylonian (*Babylonian Talmud*) schools during the Amoraic Period (third to fifth centuries A.D.). However, the term "frequently serves as a generic designation for an entire body of literature since the *Talmud* marks the culmination of the writings of Jewish tradition."[70] The tractate *Megillah*, which forms part of the Mishnaic order *Mo^{c}ed*,[71] deals primarily with the Book of Esther, but nevertheless does mention (as does the midrash *Esther Rabbah* to be examined later) both Amel-Marduk and the release of Jehoiachin. It contains the following figures for the reigns of Amel-Marduk and Nebuchadnezzar (which reportedly were determined by Belshazzar):

> It is written, 'After seventy years are accomplished for Babylon I will remember you, and it is written, that He who would accomplish for the desolation of Jerusalem seventy years.' He reckoned forty-five years of Nebuchadnezzar and twenty-three of Evil-Merodach and two of his own, making seventy in all.

Further on (after 2 Kings 25:27 is quoted) we read:

> Eight and thirty-seven makes forty-five of Nebuchadnezzar. The twenty-three of Evil-Merodach we know from tradition. These with two of his own make seventy.[72]

As we have already seen, the forty-five-year reign of Nebuchadnezzar mentioned here has at least a partial parallel in Josephus (*Jewish Antiquities*, 10. 11 2). The twenty-three-year figure for Amel-Marduk, however (which is declared to be known from tradition), occurs in no other source except the later *Seder ᶜOlam Zuta*, which probably derived it from the *Talmud*.

In addition to the *Talmud*, the midrashim, forming what is known as the *Midrash Rabbah*, contains mention of Amel-Marduk and Nebuchadnezzar. The term *midrash*, coming from the Hebrew meaning "to study" or "to investigate," was used especially to designate "exposition," "exegesis" of the Scriptures. The development of the midrash took place during three historical periods: (1) that of the Sopherim, beginning with the time of Ezra in the fifth century B.C.,[73] (2) the Tannaim; and (3) the Amoraim. Those midrashim contained in the *Midrash Rabbah* are purely haggadic in nature[74]; some were composed relatively early, others are quite late.[75] It is among these midrashim that a large portion of the information contained in Hebrew sources concerning Nebuchadnezzar can be found. As we shall see, much of what they include has its roots in Jewish tradition and can be found in the remaining Hebrew works to be discussed later.

Ten of the midrashim comprising the *Midrash Rabbah* mention Amel-Marduk or Nebuchadnezzar. They are as follows:

1. *Bereshit Rabbah*, the oldest (perhaps contemporaneous with the *Jerusalem Talmud*), which is a running commentary on the book of Genesis. It was attributed to R. Hoshaya of the third century A.D.[76]

2. *Wayikra Rabbah*, the midrash to the Book of Leviticus. This is also among the oldest midrashim. It cites as authorities both the *Pesiqta* (see below, n. 90) and *Bereshit Rabbah*.[77]

3. *Bemidbar Rabbah*, or the midrash to the Book of Numbers, is probably the youngest of the midrashim. It preserved large quantities of the *Midrash Tanhuma*, the *Talmud*, and *Wayikra Rabbah*.

4. *Koheleth Rabbah*, or the midrash to Ecclesiastes. The author and place of writing have not been determined. It largely duplicates what is contained in *Bereshit Rabbah*, *Wayikra Rabbah*, and the *Pesiqta*. This suggests another late date for its composition.[78]

5. *Shir-ha-Shirim Rabbah*, or *Midrash Hazita*, the midrash to the Song of Songs. It is one of the younger midrashim, and draws material from the *Talmud*, *Pesiqta*, *Wayikra Rabbah*, and *Bereshit Rabbah*.[79]

6. *Esther Rabbah*, a midrash to the Book of Esther composed probably in the tenth century or later. It borrows information from the *Talmud* as well as the older *Bereshit Rabbah* and *Wayikra Rabbah*.[80]

7. *Shemoth Rabbah*, or midrash to the Book of Exodus. It is a verse-by-verse commentary on the book and was composed sometime between the seventh and eleventh centuries. It probably had a limited geographical circulation. Its Aramic elements and words point to a Palestinian origin.[81]

8. *Debarim Rabbah*, or midrash to the Book of Deuteronomy. It is similar to the *Midrash Tanhuma* and was composed very late.[82]

9. *Lamentations Rabbah*, probably composed in the fourth century, contains lamentations recited in synagogues on the ninth of Ab, the date of the destruction of Jerusalem.[83]

10. *Ruth Rabbah*, dated to the sixth or seventh century, is a Palestinian midrash from the period of the Amoraim.[84]

Three of these midrashim, namely the *Bereshit*, *Wayikra*, and *Esther Rabbah*, comment extensively on the reign of Nebuchadnezzar. The *Bereshit Rabbah* relates not only the release of Jehoiachin from captivity, but also contradicts the hostile opinion of Amel-Marduk found in Berossus's *Babyloniaca*.[85] It contains one of the earliest references in any rabbinical source to Amel-Marduk as a "cosmocrator," possessed of a kingdom whose boundaries extend from one end of the world to the other.[86] The *Wayikra Rabbah* contains the first mention of the imprisonment of Amel-Marduk by Nebuchadnezzar and relates the former's fear of becoming king without first having disposed of his father's body.[87] The *Esther Rabbah*, in addition to repeating what is in the *Pesiqta* and *Bereshit Rabbah*, tells of Nebuchadnezzar's deliberate disposal of the wealth of his kingdom, thus making it impossible for Amel-Marduk to inherit it.[88] All of these stories will be dealt with more fully later.

In addition to those homiletic midrashim included in the *Midrash Rabbah*, others are "haggadic discourses on the Scripture sections intended as lessons for the feast days and special Sabbaths."[89] Two of these collections are the *Pesiqta* (mistakenly attributed to Rab Kahana and thus referred to as *Pesiqta de Rab Kahana*) and the Tanhuma midrashim. The *Pesiqta de Rab Kahana* includes homilies that are in both the Tanhuma midrashim and in *Wayikra Rabbah*. The date of its composition has been widely disputed. However, it probably should be dated to the period of composition of the *Bereshit Rabbah*. What pertinent information it contains regarding Amel-Marduk and Jehoiachin is the exact duplicate of that found in the *Esther Rabbah* already discussed, and thus probably served as a source for the midrash.[90]

The term *Tanhuma* refers to "an exegetical midrash to the Torah" and seems to be in some way connected with Rabbi Tanhuma bar Abba of the Amoraic period. Some of the homilies begin with the words "thus the Rabbi Tanhuma bar Abba began his sermon."[91] There are three groups of haggadot covering the Pentateuch that are referred to under the general heading *Midrash Tanhuma*. The first collection, called Tanhuma A (dating to the fifth century B.C.), is the oldest of the three and consists chiefly of "homilies and haggadic interpretations of the weekly sections of the Pentateuch."[92] The second (Tanhuma B, or Yelammedenu, coming from the words "let our master teach us") was probably a product of the eighth century. The *Midrash Tanhuma* in both of these collections contain mention of Amel-Marduk and Jehoiachin. It is likely that some of the information contained in the later midrashim of the *Midrash Rabbah* was drawn from the tanhumin composing these two collections.[93]

In addition to the midrashim, a number of historical works written in Hebrew have been preserved. One of these is the so-called *Seder ᶜOlam Zuta*, "named so because it follows in method and form the chronicle by that name composed by the Tanna of the second century Jose ben Halaphta."[94] It was a continuation of that older composition (the larger *Seder* ^{C}*Olam Rabbah*). This "brief order of the world" can be divided into two parts, with the first treating the fifty generations from Adam to Jehoiachin, and the second including the thirty-nine generations of exilarchs (starting with Jehoiachin). The exact date of its final writing is difficult to determine, although some authorities have seen fit to place the date somewhere in the eighth century.[95] It probably served as a source for the *Abot de Rabbi Nathan*, to be discussed shortly.[96]

Although *Seder* ^{C}*Olam Zuta* pays particular attention to the period of Jehoiachin and Amel-Marduk, very little new information emerges. It does, however, attempt to straighten out the confusion in Jeremiah 52:31 and 2 Kings 25:27 regarding the length of time spent by Jehoiachin in prison, and also deals with the confused genealogy given in 1 Chronicles 3:17-19, in which the sons of Jehoiachin are named.[97] Otherwise, the author merely repeats the story of Amel-Marduk's succession to the throne and his removal of the corpse of his father from its resting place (*Wayikra Rabbah* 18 2),[98] and also gives the same figures for the reigns of Nebuchadnezzar, Amel-Marduk, and Belshazzar contained in the *Talmud* (Megillah 11b).

Among those ethical and religious haggadot that are not part of the *Midrash Rabbah* is the *Pirke Abot* (or Sayings of the Fathers), which is incorporated into the *Mishnah*. It has a supplementary treatise known as *Abot de Rabbi Nathan*, the second recension of which contains mention of Nebuchadnezzar, Amel-Marduk, and Jehoiachin. Rabbi Nathan, who supposedly wrote the work, lived in the second century A.D., approximately a generation earlier than the editor of the *Mishnah*, Judah, the Patriarch. He could not have been the sole author of the work, however, because "several authorities are quoted who flourished a long time after R. Nathan."[99] It was probably named after him because he is one of the first authorities mentioned, but it was written in the eighth or ninth century. Much of the information contained in the two recensions is almost the exact duplicate of that included in the *Pirke Abot*, although the second recension, in some respects at least, is vastly different from the first. The author (or authors) of this latter version not only reiterates the story of the release of Jehoiachin by Amel-Marduk, told both in Scriptures and by Josephus (*Jewish Antiquities* 10. 11 2), but also includes an amplification and reinterpretation of the tale concerning the removal of Nebuchadnezzar's corpse from the grave already mentioned in *Wayikra Rabbah* and *Seder* ^{C}*Olam Zuta* 28.[100]

The last remaining Hebrew source to be accounted for is the work of a certain Jerachmeel ben Solomon (or Yerachmeel). Living in southern Italy in the twelfth century, he was the author of a *Chronicle* which, like that of Syncellus before him, paid special attention to the neo-Babylonian period. He used numerous sources, including the works of Strabo, Nicolaus of Damascus, Josippon (Yosippon, or Pseudo-Josephus), Philo, the rabbinical works (2 *Abot de Rabbi Nathan*, *Seder* *^cOlam Zuta*, and *Wayikra Rabbah*), and especially those of Josephus and Jerome.[101] In using these sources, however, he, like Syncellus, confused them. The result was not only a further alteration of what had been written before his time, but the inclusion of material (undoubtedly, the result of his own errors) that is not found in any other source.

The section of the *Chronicle* dealing specifically with Amel-Marduk includes a partial oversimplified king list, which reads as follows:

> Evil Merodach had three sons, whose names were Regosar, Lebuzer Dukh, and Nabhar, who was Belshazzar, with whom the Chaldean kingdom came to an end.[102]

The information is undoubtedly taken from Josephus (*Jewish Antiquities* 10. 11 2), although the names are badly distorted. Both Josephus and Jerachmeel equate the name Nabonidus with Belshazzar, yet Jerachmeel has further confused the arrangement by saying that Neriglissar, Labashi-Marduk, and Nabonidus were all sons of Amel-Marduk. Jerome, as will be recalled, also confused Josephus's list, but nowhere in his *Commentary on Daniel* does the equation Nabonidus = Belshazzar appear.

In addition to this, Jerachmeel borrowed from Jerome's *Commentary on Isaiah* 14:19, in which, as has already been noted, the "fable told by the Hebrews" dealing with the circumstances surrounding Amel-Marduk's accession to the throne occurs. However, in retelling it, he presents an entirely new picture of the events immediately preceding Nebuchadnezzar's death. After referring to the release of Jehoiachin, he goes on to write the following:

> He did this because Nebuchadnezzar the Great did not keep faith with him, for Evil-Merodach was really his eldest son; but he made Nebuchadnezzar the Younger king, because he had humbled the wicked. They slandered him to his father, who placed him (Evil-Merodach) in prison together with Jehoiachin, where they remained together until the death of Nebuchadnezzar, his brother after whom he reigned.[103]

These statements of Jerachmeel, especially the second relating the imprisonment of Amel-Marduk together with Jehoiachin, find only a partial parallel in the *Wayikra Rabbah* (18 2) and no parallel in any Greek or Latin source. They more likely are the result of his own reading of additional words into the *Wayikra Rabbah* and the "fable" told by Jerome.[104]

An Aramaic Source

The so-called *Prayer of Nabonidus* is an Aramaic document found three decades ago at Qumran. Although the date of this manuscript is first century B.C., it contains descriptions that are at least similar to the *Verse Account* quoted earlier. These characterizations suggest a continuity that spanned several centuries and kept alive a folkloristic image that was to be characteristic of several of the Hebrew sources, especially the Book of Daniel.

> The words of the prayer that Nabonidus, king of A(ssyria and Ba)bylon, the (great) king, prayed (when he was smitten) with a bad inflammation by the decree of the (Most High God) in (the city of) Tema. (With a bad inflammation) I was smitten for seven years and from (men) I was put away. But when I confessed my sins and my faults, He (God) allowed me (to have) a soothsayer. This was a Jewish (man of the exiles in Babylon. He) explained (it) and wrote (me) to render honor and g(reat glor)y to the name of the (Most High God. Thus he wrote: 'When) you were smitten with a b(ad) inflammation in (the city of) Tema (by the decree of the Most High God) for seven years, (you we)re praying to gods of silver and gold, (of bronze,) iron, wood, stone, (and) clay . . . that th(ese) gods . . . .'[105]

This astonishing little piece (which is, of course, midrashic in genre), identifies Nabonidus and Daniel (he must be the Jewish man of the text) and mentions Babylon and Tema — all the aspects of a historical reconstruction. This seems to indicate that the Old Testament in general, and the Book of Daniel in particular, assume far greater importance than the somewhat imaginary reconstructions found in the *Midrash Rabbah*. The point to be emphasized here is that the illness of the king and his recovery as an act of God in the *Prayer of Nabonidus* must be taken together with the traditions in Daniel and

Ahiqar as constituting the clearest set of folkloristic motifs in the sources under review.

The Apocryphal and Pseudoepigraphical Works

A number of apocryphal books written in Greek also contain mention of Nebuchadnezzar. As is the case with the Old Testament, none of these texts mentions Nabonidus. In several instances, only the name of Nebuchadnezzar occurs, with no further commentary. In others, specific reference is made to the destruction of Jerusalem and to the Captivity, with no additional remarks regarding Nebuchadnezzar as a person or king. The sources are as follows:

1. *Baruch*. Actually, this term refers to three works, the first of which is part of the Septuagint. It seemingly mentions Nebuchadnezzar in connection with Vespasian and Titus. II *Baruch* (the *Syriac Apocalypse*) refers to Nebuchadnezzar and the Captivity and the *Greek Apocalypse* (or III *Baruch*) suggests Nebuchadnezzar was permitted by God to destroy the Temple of Solomon.[106]

2. *Tobit*. This work is preserved in several languages, including Greek, Latin, and Hebrew, and was probably composed in the third century B.C. Here Nebuchadnezzar is characterized as the king of Media and is said to have taken Nineveh (a clear reference to Nabopolassar, his father).[107]

3. I *Esdras*, or the first book of the *Apocrypha*, survives in several languages, including Greek, Latin, Syriac, and Ethiopic. It includes the Old Testament story of the Captivity and names Nebuchadnezzar in relation to Cyrus.[108]

4. *Epistle of Jeremy*. This work, like the *Additions to Esther A* and *I Zadok*, contains mention of the Captivity.[109]

5. *Judith*. It survives in Greek, Latin, and Syriac versions, even though the original Hebrew is lost. It was probably composed in the second century B.C. It is, in many respects, the most interesting of the apocryphal works, because it not only refers to Nebuchadnezzar as king of Media, but it also talks of wars against Syria and Egypt. Here there seems to be an identification of the name Nebuchadnezzar with Artaxerxes Ochus, because many of the events described correspond to happenings in his reign. Nebuchadnezzar is described here as the "lord of the earth."[110]

6. The *Story of Ahiqar.* This work has cuneiform parallels (see below, chap. 6) and is folkloristic, pure and simple. It is at least as old as the fifth century B.C. and contains a characterization of an imprisoned figure that uniquely resembles the figure of Nebuchadnezzar described in Daniel (4:33).[111]

A number of these works have political overtones. As we will soon see, characterizations of Nebuchadnezzar are created that combine features of a Greek historical commentary and folkloristic elements that would have enabled the contemporary readers to identify the figure described with individual monarchs living in their own time.

Lives of the Prophets

Aside from the sources written in Greek already mentioned here, one other document is worthy of note. This is the so-called *Lives of the Prophets*, containing biographical sketches of prominent Old Testament figures. Although the authorship cannot be determined accurately, the work was probably composed near the end of the first century A.D. by someone having strong connections with or interest in Jerusalem and its history.[112] Many of the portraits included here are quite simple, but the picture of Daniel not only describes the prophet but includes a discussion of Nebuchadnezzar. The pertinent section reads as follows:

For his head and foreparts were those of an ox, his legs and hinder parts those of a lion . . . . It is the manner of tyrants, that in their youth they come under the yoke of Satan; in their latter years they become wild beasts.[113]

Here is a succinct characterization of not only Nebuchadnezzar but a tyrant as well; this "model" is embellished with folkloristic elements that clearly could be (and were) used to describe any monarch associated with achievements similar to those of Nebuchadnezzar.

The Arabic Sources

Apart from the Old Testament,[114] several sources written in Arabic mention Nebuchadnezzar. Perhaps the most interesting of these for our purposes is the *Chronology of Ancient Nations* authored by a certain

Abu-Raihan Muhammad b. 'Ahmad Albiruni (A.D. 973-1048). The work deals with "monuments or vestiges of generations of the past that have been preserved up to the author's time,"[115] and includes several king lists and tables that include the names of later Babylonian monarchs.   Much of his chronological information can be linked directly to the *Ptolemaic Canon*; however he also refers to traditions that are purely oral, even though he quite plainly denies that they have any historical value.   One of these curious traditions concerns Nebuchadnezzar (arab. Bukhtnassar) and was related by a visitor to Jerusalem.

> Alma'mun b. 'Ahmad Asalami Alharawi relates that he saw in Jerusalem some heaps of stones at a gate, called *Gate of the Column*; they had been gathered so as to form something like hills and mountains. Now people said that those were thrown over the blood of John the son of Zacharias, but that the blood rose over them, boiling and bubbling.   This went on till Nebukadnezar killed the people, and made their blood flow over it; then it was quiet.

> Of this story there is nothing in the Gospel, and I do not know what I am to say of it.   For Nebukadnezar came to Jerusalem nearly four hundred and forty-five years before the death of John; and the second destruction was the work of the Greek kings, Vespasian and Titus. But it seems that the people of Jerusalem call everybody who destroyed their town Nebukadnezar.[116]

The last statement of Albiruni, perhaps, is the most important of those found in the Arabic sources.   It best speaks to the question of relationship of culture to the characterization of a nominally historical figure.   Clearly the destruction of Jerusalem and the temple of Solomon by Nebuchadnezzar in 586 B.C. were bitter pills to swallow; in addition, the deportation to Babylon added fuel to an already kindled flame, resulting in the association of anything destructive or wicked in the Post-Exilic period with the character of Nebuchadnezzar.   To this image the Jews attached purely folkloristic elements for various purposes at various times, elements that enable the true historical figure to become lost in a picture intended to preserve the memory of the Babylonian Captivity.

Three other sources written in Arabic mention Nebuchadnezzar. They are as follows:

1. The *Tar'ikh al-Rusul w-al-Muluk* of at-Tabari, the first complete universal history in the Arabic language, arranges events chronologically from the creation to A.D. 915. At-Tabari (838-923) was born in a mountain district near the Caspian Sea. He procured some of his data from oral tradition. He mentions Nebuchadnezzar as having been with Sennacherib at Jerusalem, and as the son of Sennacherib's paternal uncle.[117]

2. The *Murudj* and *Tanbih* of Abu-al-Hasan 'Ali al-Mas'udi (d. 956), referred to as the "Herodotus of the Arabs." These were historical manuals with appendices, characterized by grouping events around dynasties, following the methodology of Ibn-Khaldun. Al-Mas'udi went from his native Baghdad to Syria and Egypt and wrote as well about Jewish history.[118]

3. The *Ma'arif* of Ibn Kutayba (born 828), a Sunni polygraph born in Kufa, who spent much time teaching in a district of Baghdad. The *Ma'arif* also was a historical manual.[119]

All of these sources preserve materials related to Nebuchadnezzar, as well as the sojourn to Tema of Nabonidus (even though the name of Nabonidus does not appear in any source).

These, then, are the sources with which one has to deal. Obviously, most of them are repetitions, and much in them is not based on historical fact. Nevertheless they reflect several cultural attitudes toward Nebuchadnezzar's achievements. The Greek and Roman writers concentrated on the building of Babylon and its fortification walls, primarily because Babylon mirrored both Athens and Rome in splendor and magnificence. The Hebrew chronicler focused instead on Nebuchadnezzar's conquest of Judah and the destruction of the temple of Solomon, because the taking of Jerusalem had to be remembered as an act never to be repeated. Images, therefore, of both a conqueror and a builder emerged to preserve memory of both the positive and negative accomplishments of Nebuchadnezzar for generations to come.

4

Nebuchadnezzar the Destroyer

Although the Babylonian scribe traditionally portrayed his monarch as a devotee of Marduk who maintained or restored sanctuaries and beautified the capital city, there was another side to his character. As we discovered in the Introduction, not all was peace and harmony, at least at the beginning of Nebuchadnezzar's reign. His father Nabopolassar had to deal with numerous Aramean tribes, no less than the Egyptians; problems on the western frontier continued to plague Nebuchadnezzar, and he had to devote a portion of his time to military campaigns. Unfortunately, the important Babylonian accounts of much of this activity either await publication or have yet to be discovered; consequently, the following account may appear disjointed to the general readers trying to acquaint themselves with Nebuchadnezzar's military activities from a "primary source" point of view. Yet the present fragmentary condition of the *Babylonian Chronicle* can lead to virtually no other alternative. Because the historical Nebuchadnezzar is so elusive, we should look instead at his later images, about which we can say much more, and that is the primary reason for this inquiry. Pieces of a rather large puzzle can be found in such diverse works as the *Babyloniaca* of Berossus, the *Jewish Antiquities* of Josephus, and the writings of at-Tabari, all of which emphasize what conquest meant to various people in different time periods. To the Babylonian chronicler, mere mention of an event occurring in a particular year was almost always sufficient. On the other hand, to the Jews living in Palestine or the Seleucids of the Hellenistic Age, the victories won (or defeats suffered) by Nebuchadnezzar's armies in many cases were events of major importance to be examined in great detail. Then the image of the conqueror became as important as the conquest itself, and the image of the conqueror had to be shaped by the actual historical event and its consequences for that culture. The result, in Nebuchadnezzar's case, was a distortion of fact that could be applied to other aspects of the king's reign as well. Let us begin, then, with the surviving fragments of the *Babylonian Chronicle* and try to determine the extent of Nebuchadnezzar's military campaigns in his early years.

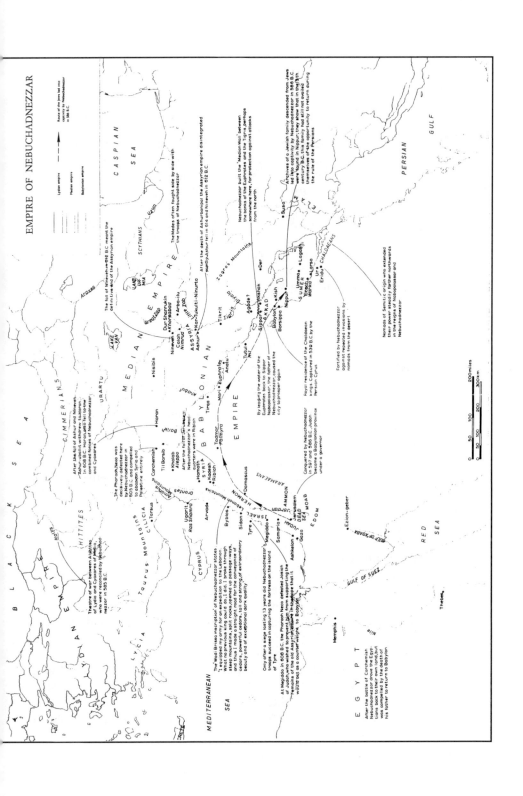

EMPIRE OF NEBUCHADNEZZAR

Lydian empire

Median empire

Babylonian empire

Route of the Jews led into captivity by Nebuchadnezzar in 586 B.C.

The fall of Nineveh in 612 B.C. meant the definitive end of the Assyrian empire

The Medes often fought side by side with the troops of Nebuchadnezzar

After the death of Ashurbanipal the Assyrian empire disintegrated rapidly. Ashur fell in 614 and Nineveh in 612 B.C.

Nebuchadnezzar built the "Median Wall" between the banks of the Euphrates and the Tigris, perhaps somewhere here, for protection against attacks from the north.

Archives of a Jewish family descended from Jews led into captivity by Nebuchadnezzar in 586 B.C. were found in Nippur; they show that in the 5th century B.C. this family had still not availed themselves of the opportunity to return during the rule of the Persians

After the fall of Ashur and Nineveh Ashur-uballit withdrew to Harran. In 608 B.C. Harran also fell to the combined forces of Nebuchadnezzar and Cyaxares

The Pharaoh Neco was decisively defeated here by Nebuchadnezzar in 605 B.C. and compelled to abandon Syria and Palestine entirely

After the battle at Carchemish Nebuchadnezzar's headquarters were in Riblah

By leading the water of the Euphrates back to Sippar Nabopolassar, the father of Nebuchadnezzar, caused the city to prosper again

Royal residence of the Chaldean kings. Captured in 539 B.C. by the Persian Cyrus.

Conquered by Nebuchadnezzar in 597 and 586 B.C. Judah became a Babylonian province under a governor

Fortified by Nebuchadnezzar against repeated invasions by nomads from the desert

Nomads of Semitic origin who extended their power steadily further northwards in the reigns of Nabopolassar and Nebuchadnezzar

The Wadi Brisa inscription of Nebuchadnezzar states "I equipped my army for an expedition to the Lebanon. What no previous king could do, I did. I broke through steep mountains, split rocks, opened up passage-ways, and thus I made a straight road for the conveyance of cedars, powerful cedars, tall and strong, of extraordinary beauty and of exceptional dark quality."

Only after a siege lasting 13 years did Nebuchadnezzar's troops succeed in capturing the fortress on the island of Tyre

At Megiddo in 608 B.C. the Pharaoh Neco defeated Josiah of Judah, who wished to prevent Juin from supporting the remains of the old Assyrian state in Harran. In Europe, that is, wanted Neco as a counterweight to Babylon.

After the battle of Carchemish Nebuchadnezzar drove the Egyptians back to their own land, but was compelled by the death of his father to return to Babylon.

Theatre of war between Alyattes of Lydia and Cyaxares of Media, who were reconciled by Nebuchadnezzar in 585 B.C.

BLACK SEA

MEDIA

LYDIA

HITTITES

PHRYGIA

CIMMERIANS

URARTU

LAKE VAN

SCYTHIANS

ARARAT

CASPIAN SEA

USUS

MEDIAN EMPIRE

Zagros Mountains

Amanus Mountains

Taurus Mountains

CILICIA

Tarsus

CYPRUS

CRETE

MEDITERRANEAN SEA

Ugarit
Ras Shamra

Arvad

Byblos

Sidon

Tyre

Megiddo

Samaria

Jerusalem

Gaza

Ashkelon

ISRAEL

JUDAH

DEAD SEA

MOAB

EDOM

AMMON

Jordan

HERMON

Lebanon Mountains

Damascus

Tadmor
Palmyra

Hamath
Kadesh
Riblah

Khalab
Aleppo

Til Barsib

Carchemish

Harran

Orontes

Balih

Euphrates

Mari

Khabur

Tirqa

Andu

BABYLONIAN EMPIRE

SYRIA

ARAMAEANS

Tikrit

Nineveh
Calah
Nimrud

Dur Sharrukin
Khorsabad

Arba-ilu

ASSYRIA
Kar-Tukulti-Ninurta

Kar-ilu
Zab

Tigris

Agade?

Sippar

AKKAD

Kutha
Babylon
Borsippa

Kish

Nippur

Umma
Erech
Uruk
Warka

Lagash

Larsa

SUMER

Eridu

Ur

CHALDEANS

Der

Susa

PERSIAN GULF

RED SEA

GULF OF SUEZ

GULF OF AQABA

Ezion-geber

EGYPT

Nile

Memphis

Thebes

0   50   100   200 miles
0   50   100   200   300 km

To the West of the Euphrates – Syria and Egypt

As D. J. Wiseman has noted, it is extremely difficult to pinpoint Nebuchadnezzar's exact location at the time of his father's death.[1] What is certain is that he had to return to the capital city to take Nabopolassar's place as "king of Babylon." After he was crowned, he could return to the west to attend to considerable unfinished business. Before he ascended to the throne, Nebuchadnezzar had already established a considerable reputation as a field commander. In fact, in early 605 B.C. he had taken the initiative against the Egyptian armies located south of Carchemish on the Euphrates River after Nabopolassar's return to Babylon.[2] A decisive battle ensued, and the *Babylonian Chronicle* recorded the details of the important Chaldean victory with the following words:

[The twenty-first year]:   The king of Akkad stayed home while Nebuchadnezzar, his eldest son (and) crown prince, mustered [the army of Akkad]. He took his army's lead and marched to Carchemish which is on the bank of the Euphrates. He crossed the river [*to encounter the army of Egypt*] which was encamped at Carchemish.[. . .]They did battle together. The army of Egypt retreated before him. He inflicted a [defeat] upon them and finished them off completely. In the district of Hamath the army of Akkad overtook the remainder of the army of [Egypt which] managed to escape [from] the defeat and which was not overcome. They (the army of Akkad) inflicted a defeat upon them (so that) a single (Egyptian) man [did not return] home. At that time Nebuchadnezzar (II) conquered all of Ha[ma]th.[3]

Almost immediately after formally ascending his father's throne, Nebuchadnezzar found himself again in Syria in an attempt to subdue a number of small areas – a likely consequence of the battle of Carchemish itself.[4]   Several cities apparently accepted Chaldean suzerainty – among them Sidon, Tyre, and Damascus, and the noted Jehoiachin of Judah became a vassal as well.[5] Harsher measures had to be taken against others, most notably Askelon, which had to be destroyed. "He marched to *Ashkelon*," says the chronicler, "and in the month of Kislev he captured it, seized its king, plundered [and sac]ked it. He turned the city into a ruin heap. In the month Shebat he marched away and [returned] to Bab[ylon]," having secured the allegiance of "all the kings of Hatti."[6]

Despite the fragmentary condition of some of the *Babylonian Chronicle* at this point, it is clear that for the next three or so years Nebuchadnezzar campaigned in Syria where his local officials were engaged in collecting tribute.[7] It is obvious that Egypt remained a thorn in Nebuchadnezzar's side, because the entry for 601 mentions a skirmish between his forces and those of Necho II (610-595 B.C.) that stood in his way. "They fought one another," the chronicler writes, "in the battlefield and both sides suffered severe losses (lit., they inflicted a major defeat upon one another). The king of Akkad and his army turned and [went back] to Babylon."[8] He spent the next year (600-599) in his capital city, licking his wounds from the Egyptian encounter, after which he returned to Syria to campaign once again. Here the chronicler notes that some of his troops "plundered extensively the possessions, animals and gods of the numerous Arabs" of the desert.[9] Such a practice was not uncommon. Several Assyrian monarchs of the preceding century had done the same thing for security reasons, and Nebuchadnezzar needed to hold such territory if he were ever to overcome successfully the stubborn Egyptian resistance on the western horizon. Finally, "in the month of Adar" (598 B.C.) "the king went home".[10]

The Classical Sources

Thus far, we have been examining only the cuneiform accounts of Nebuchadnezzar's early years. Despite their frankness, they obviously leave much unsaid. What did the Egyptian sources have to say? Are the accounts in the Old Testament the only other extant sources for the events outlined above? Surely (as noted in chapter 2), other descriptions reflecting different cultural attitudes toward the same campaigns must have existed. Unfortunately, little of this material survives. Not until we reach the writings of the Hellenistic and Roman authors do additional pictures emerge of Nebuchadnezzar and his campaigns into Syria and against Egypt. Nevertheless, these later Greek and Latin sources are important (considering the questions raised in this investigation) and require some comments and analysis here.

Berossus and Megasthenes

Few of the Greek and Latin sources surviving antiquity contain any mention of Nebuchadnezzar's early years. This may be the result of a lack of interest in such a subject shown by the audiences these commentaries were intended to address. In a broader sense, however, it also may reflect a focus on something other than conquest, because "universal" histories of the classical and Hellenistic authors tended to concentrate on achievements that endured beyond any particular individual's lifetime. Whatever the case, when we examine the relevant sections of the works of Berossus and Megasthenes (written in the Seleucid period), we find in one an account similar to that contained in the *Babylonian Chronicle*, and in the other a somewhat "nationalistic" characterization of Nebuchadnezzar[11] as a sort of "world monarch." To begin with, Berossus describes the events immediately preceding the death of Nabopolassar:

> Nabopalassaros, his father, heard that the satrap who had been posted to Egypt, Coele, Syria, and Phoenicia, had become a rebel. No longer himself equal to the task, he entrusted a portion of his army to his son Nabouchodonosoros, who was still in the prime of life, and sent him against the rebel. Nabouchodonosoros drew up his force in battle order and engaged the rebel. He defeated him and subjected the country to the rule of the Babylonians again. At this very time Nabopalassaros, his father, fell ill and died in the city of the Babylonians after having been king for twenty-one years.[12]

Nebuchadnezzar immediately made arrangements to return to the capital, taking prisoners with him from the campaign against Necho:

> Nabouchodonosoros learned of his father's death shortly thereafter. After he arranged affairs in Egypt and the remaining territory, he ordered some of his friends to bring the Jewish, Phoenician, Syrian and Egyptian prisoners together with the bulk of the army and the rest of the booty to Babylonia. He himself set out with a few companions and reached Babylon by crossing the desert. On finding that affairs were being managed by the Chaldeans and the kingship being maintained by the noblest one of these, he took charge of the whole of his father's realm. When the prisoners arrived, he ordered that dwelling places be assigned to them in the most suitable parts of Babylonia.[13]

How dramatically different this information is when compared with the decidedly fantastic account of the Seleucid envoy to India,

Megasthenes, who sought to equate Nebuchadnezzar's achievements with those of a superhuman:

> That Nabucodrosorus [Nebuchadnezzar], having become more powerful than Hercules, invaded Libya and Iberia, [Spain], and when he had rendered them tributary, he extended his conquests over the inhabitants of the shores upon the right of the sea.[14]

Eddy pointed out years ago that the place names included in these accounts reflect a Seleucid interest in the area of Syria, Palestine, and Egypt.[15] Hence, it should not be surprising to find Nebuchadnezzar's name appearing in Berossus's *Babyloniaca*, because he campaigned in these areas. Yet although this description survives "third hand" (from Josephus through Alexander Polyhistor) with little indication of what the whole *Babyloniaca* originally contained, there is enough here to suggest no preoccupation with a "conqueror image." Information considered factual to Berossus was seemingly included not for the purpose of glorifying conquest. Instead, it served merely as background material for the really important characterization of the builder of Babylon itself.

The Jewish Antiquities

Apart from the few references in the Old Testament to Nebuchadnezzar's campaigns against Egypt, only one other writer, Josephus, comments extensively on this period. His *Jewish Antiquities* includes an account of the battle of Carchemish. Although the problem of sources used remains largely unresolved,[16] the relationship between Judah and the Chaldean kingdom in the seventh and sixth centuries B.C. was clearly a topic of great interest to Josephus. Not only does much of his narrative incorporate huge sections of the Book of Daniel, but his account of the initial campaigns into Syria and Palestine also suggests an acquaintance with Jewish folklore that ultimately kept alive an animosity toward the architect of the Babylonian Captivity. To begin with, the details of the encounter with the forces of Necho II in 605 B.C. are presented:

> In the fourth year of his reign someone called Nebuchadnezzar became ruler of the Babylonians and at the same time went up with a great armament

against the city of Karchamissa—this is on the Euphrates river—with the determination to make war on the Egyptian king Nechao, to whom all Syria was subject. When Nechao learned of the Babylonian king's purpose and of the expedition against him, he himself did not show indifference but set out for the Euphrates with a large force to oppose Nebuchadnezzar. In the engagement that took place he was defeated and lost many myriads in the battle. Then the Babylonian king crossed the Euphrates and occupied all Syria, with the exception of Judaea, as far as Pelusium.[17]

Despite his acquaintance with the *Babyloniaca* of Berossus,[18] the rather jumbled chronology of events presented here suggests a reliance on a Jewish oral tradition having its roots in the period immediately after the destruction of the temple of Solomon by Nebuchadnezzar in 586 B.C. Josephus was a native of the area whose history he records. Considering the overall purpose of the *Jewish Antiquities*, it should hardly be surprising to find that it includes the description of a Babylonian conqueror cited above.

Following this, however, is an interesting account of the imposition of tribute on Jehoiachim, king of Judah, who (contrary to the advice of the prophet Jeremiah)[19] had relied on continued help from Egypt. In relating his information, Josephus includes an account of both the prophecy of Jeremiah concerning the destruction of Jerusalem and his imprisonment at the hands of Jehoiachim. After Jeremiah's release from prison, Josephus explains,

He then wrote down all his prophecies and, while the people kept a fast and were assembled in the temple, in the ninth month of the fifth year of the reign of Joakeimos, he read the book which he had composed concerning the things which were to befall the city and the temple and the people. But when the leaders heard it, they took the book from him and ordered both him and his scribe Baruch to take themselves off and not let themselves be seen by anyone; as for the book, they carried it off and gave it to the king. And he, in the presence of his friends, ordered his scribe to take it and read it aloud. But, when he heard what was in the book, the king became angry and destroyed it by tearing it apart and throwing it into the fire. Then he ordered that a search be made for both Jeremiah and his scribe Baruch and that they be brought to him for punishment. So then they escaped his wrath.[20]

No mention of any campaign against Judah is recorded in the *Babylonian Chronicle* before Nebuchadnezzar's seventh year (597 B.C.). Furthermore, the chronology in both the Hebrew and Greek texts of the book of Jeremiah is hopelessly confused. Josephus may have relied on information gathered from Alexander Polyhistor for his account of events occurring immediately before the destruction of Jerusalem. However, the description quoted above, as well as the material that follows, demonstrates again a reliance on a well established local tradition that had already cast Nebuchadnezzar in a negative light.[21] Thus while the classical and Hellenistic Greek writers viewed conquest as having relatively minor significance (see below, chap. 6), Hebrew written and oral tradition considered it to be quite different, as the subsequent accounts of the destruction of Solomon's temple show clearly.

Nebuchadnezzar and the Kingdom of Judah

With characteristic brevity, the *Babylonian Chronicle* records the activities of Nebuchadnezzar's seventh year, the year of the attack on the kingdom of Judah and the first deportation of captives to Babylon:

The seventh year: In the month Kislev the king of Akkad mustered his army and marched to Hattu. He encamped against the city of Judah and on the second day of the month Adar he captured the city (and) seized (its) king. A king of his own choice he appointed in the city (and) taking the vast tribute he brought it back to Babylon.[22]

Wiseman's initial publication of BM 21946 provided, finally, confirmation of an exact date of the siege of Jerusalem (16 March 597 B.C.). Jehoiachim, the former king of Judah, had died before the campaign,[23] and Jehoiachin, the occupant of the throne when Nebuchadnezzar arrived, was removed and replaced by Zedekiah, the former king's uncle.[24] Josephus, in recounting these events, relates information that has no parallel in the Scriptures. Nevertheless, similar words can be found in later rabbinic literature:

Joachimos, who succeeded him on the throne, had a mother named Nooste, a native of the city, and reigned three months and ten days.

But after the Babylonian king had given the kingdom to Joachimos, a sudden fear seized him, for he was afraid that Joachimos might bear him a grudge for the killing of his father, and lead his country to revolt. He therefore sent a force which besieged Joachimos in Jerusalem. But he, being kind and just, did not think it right to suffer the city to be endangered on his account, and removed his mother and his relatives and delivered them to the commanders sent by the Babylonian king, after receiving their oath that neither these nor the city should suffer any harm. But their pledge was not kept for even as long as a year, for the Babylonian king did not observe it, but commanded his men to take captive all the young men and craftsmen in the city and bring them in chains to him—these came to ten thousand eight hundred and thirty-two in all—as well as Joachimos with his mother and friends. And, when they had been brought to him, he kept them under guard, and appointed Joachimos' uncle Sacchias as king, after receiving his oath that he would surely keep the country for him and attempt no uprising nor show friendliness to the Egyptians.

Now Sacchias was twenty-one years old when he took over royal power, and he was a brother of Joakeimos by the same mother but he was contemptuous of justice and duty, for those of his own age about him were impious, and the entire multitude had licence to act as outrageously as it pleased. For it was this reason that the prophet Jeremiah came to him and solemnly protested, bidding him leave off his various impieties and lawless acts, and watch over justice and neither pay heed to the leaders, because there were wicked men among them, or put faith in the false prophets who were deceiving him by saying that the Babylonian king would never again make war on the city and that the Egyptians would take the field against the Babylonian king and conquer him.[25]

The first section of this description has at least a partial parallel in Eupolemus, who says he derived his information from Alexander Polyhistor[26]:

Then Jonacheim ruled. At this time the prophet Jeremiah prophesied. Sent by God, he caught the Jews sacrificing to a golden idol whose name was Baal. He declared to them the coming misfortune. Jonacheim attempted to burn him alive, but Jeremiah said that with that very timber they would prepare food for the Babylonians and that as captives they should dig the trenches of the Tigris and Euphrates. When Nebuchadnezzar the king of the Babylonians heard what was being prophesied by Jeremiah, he called upon Astibares, the king of the Medes, to join him in making war. Using the

Babylonians and the Medes, after he gathered 180,000 foot soldiers, he first subdued Samaria, Galilee, Scythopolis, and the Jews living in Gilead. Then he took Jerusalem and captured alive Jonacheim the king of the Jews. After he had taken as tribute the gold in the temple, as well as the silver and the (!) bronze, he transported it to Babylon without the ark and the tablets which it contained. These Jeremiah withheld.[27]

These accounts suggest that a rich body of folklore existed at the time Josephus wrote *Jewish Antiquities*. More than five centuries had passed since Cyrus II of Persia had allowed the Jews to return to their homeland. The experiences of nearly a half century of captivity had to be kept alive and passed down from one generation to another. The dry event-by-event entries of the kind found in the *Babylonian Chronicle* simply could not serve this purpose. Narratives had to be embellished with elements that could fashion a sort of hellenic tale combining the factual with the didactic,[28] the entertaining with the fantastic, to best keep alive the memory of the Babylonian Captivity. However, the accounts we have examined thus far only touched upon the consequences of the battle of Carchemish and the deportations connected with the siege of Jerusalem in 597 B.C. Although we can see evolving here an image of a conqueror-king whose deeds would eventually be avenged through conquest of the entire Chaldean kingdom, a more complete characterization had to await the results of yet another campaign into Judah. The second campaign of 586 B.C., although still undocumented in the cuneiform sources, lives vividly in the verses of the Old Testament, in the *Jewish Antiquities*, and in the rabbinic commentaries reflecting the oral tradition upon which Josephus's narrative must have been based. The true reason for the negative image of Nebuchadnezzar will emerge from these sources—one connected not so much with deportation, but with the destruction of the temple of Solomon.

Nebuchadnezzar and the Rabbinic Commentaries

Neither the *Babylonian Chronicle* nor most of the writings of the Greek historians and chronographers mention Nebuchadnezzar's second campaign. The Old Testament, apart from the books of Daniel and Jeremiah (discussed in more detail in chapter 6), gives us only the barest outline of the event. However Josephus, in his *Jewish Antiquities*, relates not only the prophecies of Ezekiel[29] and Jeremiah,[30] along with the details of Zedekiah's breaking his alliance with Nebuchadnezzar[31] in favor of Egypt,[32] but he also provides the following description of the siege of Jerusalem in 586 B.C.:

Now the Babylonian king applied himself very strenuously and zealously to the siege of Jerusalem; he built towers on great earthworks from which he kept back those stationed on the walls, and also erected round the whole circuit (of the city) many earthworks equal in height to the walls. But those within bore the siege with courage and spirit, for they did not weaken under either famine or disease, but, although plagued internally by these afflictions, opposed stout hearts to the war; neither were they dismayed at the devices and engines of their foes, but on their side devised engines to check all those used by the enemy so that the contest between the Babylonians and the people of Jerusalem was wholly one of cleverness and skill, one side thinking that the capture of the city could be more easily affected in this way, while the other placed its hope of deliverance solely in not wearying or giving up the search for counter-devices by which the engines of their foes might be rendered useless. And thus they held out for eighteen months until they were exhausted by the famine and by the missiles which the enemy hurled at them from the towers.

The city was taken in the eleventh year of the reign of Sacchias, on the ninth day of the fourth month.[33]

Josephus continues on (in his *Against Apion*) to relate Berossus's comments on the destruction of Solomon's temple:

In his narrative of the actions of this monarch he relates how he sent his son Nabuchodonosor with a large army to Egypt and to our country, on hearing that these people had revolted, and how he defeated them all, burnt the temple at Jerusalem, dislodged and transported our entire population to Babylon, with the result that the city lay desolate for seventy years until the time of Cyrus, king of Persia.[34]

A more complete description of the destruction of Jerusalem can be found in the *Apocrypha*, in which we read this account:

So after a year Nabuchodonosor sent and caused him to be brought into Babylon with the holy vessels of the Lord; and made Sedekias king of Judaea and Jerusalem, when he was one and twenty years old; and he reigned eleven years: and he also did evil in the sight of the Lord, and cared not for the words that were spoken by Jeremy the prophet from the mouth of the Lord. And after that king Nabuchodonosor had made him to swear by the name of the Lord, he forswore himself, and rebelled; and hardening his neck, and his heart he transgressed the laws of the Lord the God of Israel. Moreover the governors of the people and of the priests did many things wickedly, and passed all the pollutions of all nations, and defiled the temple of the Lord, which was sanctified in Jerusalem. And the God of their fathers sent by his messenger to call them back, because he had compassion on them and on his dwelling place.

But they mocked his messengers; and in the day when the Lord spake *unto them*, they scoffed at his prophets: so far forth, that he, being wroth with his people for their great ungodliness, commanded to bring up the kings of the Chaldeans against them, who slew their young men with the sword, round about their holy temple, and spared neither young man nor maid, old man nor child; but he delivered all into their hands. And they took all the holy vessels of the Lord, both great and small, with the vessels of the ark of the Lord, and the king's treasures, and carried them away unto Babylon. And they burnt the house of the Lord, and broke down the walls of Jerusalem, and burnt the towers thereof with fire: and as for her glorious things, they never ceased till they had brought them all to nought: and the people that were not slain with the sword he carried unto Babylon: and they were servants unto him and to his children, till the Persians reigned, to fulfill the word of the Lord by the mouth of Jeremy: Until the land hath enjoyed her sabbaths, the whole time of her desolation shall she keep sabbath, to fulfill threescore and ten years.[35]

By the time the Babylonian Captivity ended in 538 B.C., a wealth of information was available concerning the experiences of the Hebrews in Babylonia. Those fortunate enough to return to Palestine passed the memory of the Exile on (in written or oral form) to succeeding generations. Many centuries later, the rabbis responsible for the *Talmud*, the *Midrash Rabbah*, and other Hebrew secondary literature translated this knowledge of the reigns of Nebuchadnezzar and his successors into images of unbridled arrogance and destruction that could be, in turn, applied to anyone who dared repeat these deeds. The imprisonment of Jehoiachin, the deportation of the Hebrews into Babylonia, and the dismantling of Solomon's temple were events easily transformed and associated with the characterization of a "cosmocrator"[36] whose empire had no limits and whose destructive acts would one day be avenged. But there was more than this. To further enhance the negative side of Nebuchadnezzar, the rabbis contrasted his reign with that of his son Amel-Marduk, who is said to have released Jehoiachin from prison after he ascended to the throne.

In the process, the Hebrew sources were able to stress both the "positive" and "negative" aspects of the Babylonian Captivity and to incorporate both into an essentially didactic treatise.

According to Jewish legend, Nebuchadnezzar spent seven years "among the beasts,"[37] during which time high state officials took Amel-Marduk and made him king in his father's place. However, Nebuchadnezzar returned and subsequently threw his son into prison for life, holding him responsible for this act of infidelity.[38] These events prompted Amel-Marduk to refuse the throne the second time it was offered, saying "I shall not heed you; the first time, after I hearkened to you, he took me and imprisoned me, the next time he will slay me."[39] It was only after Nebuchadnezzar's corpse was dragged from its resting place through the streets of Babylon that Amel-Marduk would ascend the throne.

A completely different version of this story is given by Jerome in his *Commentary on Isaiah* 14:19 and in the *Chronicle* of Jerachmeel. Jerome states that the fear that Amel-Marduk would succeed his father rested with the "magnates of the state"[40] and not with the new king himself. They were fearful of a reappearance of Nebuchadnezzar and would not allow the son to become king. This story, which Jerome calls "a fable told by the Hebrews," does not appear earlier or in the later rabbinical works. It was probably borrowed by Jerachmeel, who not only adds that Nebuchadnezzar the Younger (i.e., the brother of Amel-Marduk) succeeded his father to the throne, but also asserts for the first time that it was the Jewish king Jehoiachin who advised Amel-Marduk (after his brother's death and his release from prison) to drag his father's corpse out of the grave. As he writes,

Now, in the thirty-seventh year of the captivity of Jehoiachin, king of Judah, on the twenty-seventh day of the twelfth month Evil-Merodach, king of Babylon, in the first year of his reign, rescued Jehoiachin, king of Judah, from prison, and raised his throne above that of any other king in Babylon, and, changing his prison garments, he maintained him as long as he lived. He did this because Nebuchadnezzar the Great did not keep his faith with him, for Evil Merodach was really his eldest son; but he made Nebuchadnezzar the Younger king, because he had humbled the wicked. They slandered him to his father, who placed him (Evil Merodach) in prison together with Jehoiachin, where they remained together until the death of Nebuchadnezzar, his brother after whom he reigned. "I fear my father Nebuchadnezzar," he said, "lest he rise from his grave, for just as he was changed back from an animal to a man, so in the same manner he may rise up from death to life." But Jehoiachin advised him to take the corpse out of the grave, and, cutting it into 300 pieces, to give it to 300 vultures, and he said to him, 'thy father will not rise up until these vultures have brought back the flesh of they father, which they have eaten."[41]

According to Josephus[42] and 2 *Abot de Rabbi Nathan*, Amel-Marduk wished to release Jehoiachin from prison because he felt he had been held by his father without cause. However, high state officials were upset by this, saying "a king cannot revoke the edicts of his dead predecessor, unless he drags the corpse of the dead king out of the grave,"[43] which is why Amel-Marduk proceeded hastily to remove his father's body. After the act was done, Jehoiachin, who, according to 2 Chronicles 36:9, "had done evil in the sight of the Lord,"[44] was immediately set at liberty and given an allowance. "Do not feel grieved," said Amel-Marduk, "at having been a prisoner this long time; forget not that thy captor was a king like thee, and not an ordinary man; to avenge the injustice done by him to thee, I dishonored his dead body."[45] According to *Esther Rabbah*, this act was also partly motivated by Nebuchadnezzar's disposal of his kingdom's wealth before his death.[46] Thus the Hebrew sources present a portrayal of a king who was not only hated for his destructive acts by the Jews, but was despised by the Chaldeans as well.

Nebuchadnezzar's Later Years

Comments in the *Babylonian Chronicle* on the years after 597 B.C. relate details of still more expeditions into Syria. Portions of these accounts are fragmentary, but there are at least token indications of problems arising with Elam and perhaps an enemy on the upper Tigris.[47] After the entry for the tenth year (when the king remained in Babylonia for part of the year),[48] the chronicle breaks off. However, in recounting (from Phoenician sources)[49] the siege of Tyre early in Nebuchadnezzar's reign, Josephus makes it quite plain that problems with Egypt persisted.[50] Although we are still uncertain how these difficulties were resolved, a fragmentary cuneiform text, now in the British Museum, hints at a campaign around 570 B.C. against the Saite king Amasis:

. . .[in] the 37th year, Nebuchadnezzar, king of Bab[ylon] mar[ched against] Egypt (Mi-sir) to deliver a battle. [Ama]sis (Text: [. . .] -a(?) -su), of Egypt, [called up his a]rm[y] . . . [. . .]ku from the town *Putu-*

Iaman. . .distant regions which (are situated on islands) amidst the sea . . . many . . . which/who (are) in Egypt . . . [car]rying weapons, horses and [chariot]s . . . he called up to assist him and. . .did [. . .] in front of him. . .he put his trust. . .[51]

This would, perhaps, be as far as we could go with a commentary on Nebuchadnezzar's conquests were it not for an interesting account of an expedition into Arabia found in the writings of at-Tabari. Earlier we noted[52] that several Assyrian kings had campaigned in Arabia, and even the *Babylonian Chronicle* suggests that some of Nebuchadnezzar's troops found their way there in his early years.[53] But at-Tabari relates the following sequence of events:

I was told on the authority of Hisham b. Muhammad that he said: The beginning of the settling of the Arab in the land of Iraq and their dwelling there and their taking al-hirah and al-'anbar as dwelling places according to what was mentioned to us, and Allah knows best, was that Allah, the Mighty and the Powerful, inspired Barakhya [?] b. {???} b. Zarbabil [? Serubabelis???] b. [Shalti'il ?]Shaltil b. Yehudha. [Hisham said, on the authority of Ash-Sharqi, Shaltil was the first of those to take at-tafshil] Go to Bukht Nasr and command him to raid against the ^cArab who did not lock their houses or their doors and trample their country under foot with an army and kill their warriors and seize their wealth as booty and make known their ingratitude to me and their taking gods other than me and their denying my prophets and messengers. So Barakhya came from Najran until he arrived at Bukht Nasr in Babylon, and he was Nabukhadh Nasr and the Arabs arabized it, and he told him what Allah had inspired in him and narrated what He had ordered, and that was in the time of Ma^cadd b. ^cAdnan. So Bukht Nasr fell on those Arab traders who were in his country. They used to come to them with merchandise and goods and get provisions of grain, dates, clothing, etc. from them. He gathered whom he seized of them and built an enclosure for them on a hill and fortified it. Then he collected them in it and set up guards over them and watched them. Then he announced the raid to the people and they got ready for it.

The news got out among the Arabs who were in the status of clients, and groups of them submitted to him [or, became Muslims], seeking safety. Bukht Nasr asked Barakhya for advice, and he said, "If their coming to you from their land is before your going out against them, what they had should be returned to them. Receive them and treat them well." So Bukht Nasr settled them in the arable areas on the banks of the Euphrates, and they built a place for their armies, which some call al-Anbar. He left the people of al-hirah alone, and they took it as a home during the life of Bukht Nasr. When he died, they joined forces with the people of al-Anbar, and the remains of the enclosure fell into ruin.[54]

Nothing like this account is to be found in any other source. It is, however, strangely reminiscent of the events transpiring during the seventh through the tenth years of Nabonidus, who forsook his kingdom for a sojourn to Tema.[55] The Jews of the Post Exilic period were familiar with that tradition and made ample use of it in describing the madness of Nebuchadnezzar in the Book of Daniel. It also found its way into the *Lives of the Prophets* where there can be no mistaking the origin of the characterization of "Nebuchadnezzar the destroyer" with the historic Nabonidus:

He made great supplication in behalf of Nebuchadnezzar whose son Belshazzar besought him for aid at the time when the king became a beast of the field, lest he should perish. For his head and foreparts were those of an ox, his legs and hinder parts those of a lion. The meaning of this marvel was revealed to the prophet: the king became a beast because of his self indulgence and his stubbornness. It is the manner of tyrants, that in their youth they come under the yoke of Satan; in their latter years they become wild beasts, snatching, destroying smiting, and slaying.[56]

The opening paragraphs of this chapter suggested that conquest meant many things to different people. As we have just seen, the image of the conqueror had to be dictated by the actual historical event and the impact it had on any particular culture. The result was a cultural distortion of fact that would not be totally confined to conquest. As we will see in the following pages, such a "fictional" characterization could also be applied to the creator of enduring monuments, as Nebuchadnezzar was in Babylon itself.

5

Nebuchadnezzar the Builder

Babylon lies in a wide plain, a vast city in the form of a square with sides nearly fourteen miles long, and a circuit of some fifty-six miles, and in addition to its enormous size it surpasses in splendour any city of the known world. It is surrounded by a broad deep moat full of water, and within the moat there is a wall fifty royal cubits wide and two hundred high.

−Herodotus, *Histories*, bk. 1., 179

When the "father of history" composed this famous description of Babylon, the Chaldean dynasty was a thing of the past. Gobbled up by the aggressive Persians, the whole of Mesopotamia had become but a small portion of an empire that was to stretch from India to the doorstep of the Aegean. Nevertheless, while the wars between Athens, Sparta, and the Persian Empire were the primary focus of Herodotus's *Histories*, space was provided for more than just a few stories about the achievements of several kingdoms that by 425 B.C. had ceased to exist. The reason for this is obvious. Although Greece, by our travel standards today, was only a stone's throw from Turkey or Egypt, few, if any, could afford to travel there to view the wonders of antiquity that constituted part of the legacy of the ancient Near East. The metropolitan centers of Egypt and Mesopotamia that served as the focal points of all economic and religious activity were far removed from the Athens of the age of Pericles. Yet these centers were characterized by the same monumental architecture and sculpture that were found in Athens; they were the source of the pride reflected later in the famous Periclean Oration of Thucydides. Other authors of "universal histories" in classical times sought to include mention of cities and temples of imposing size while idolizing the individuals responsible for them. As a result, tales of Babylon and its famous Hanging Gardens turned up everywhere; only a monarch of god-like dimensions could possibly have created such marvels. Fortunately for us, the spade of the archaeologist has turned up not only remains of the Babylon of

Chaldean times but also the original accounts of construction projects undertaken during the reign of Nebuchadnezzar. Although the emphasis on the "superhuman" element is missing from these records, the fulfillment of a traditional obligation of Babylonian kings most certainly is not. Nebuchadnezzar was the vicar of Marduk on earth; his capital city had to be fortified and beautified in accordance with his god's will. Because of the extent of the campaigns against Judah, Phoenicia, and Egypt, these building projects required several years to complete. The results of these efforts, however, were impressive. They served as adequate praise of the "king of the gods" and immortalized Nebuchadnezzar (albeit in abstract form) in the histories of Herodotus and his classical contemporaries. Let us then look first at Babylon through contemporary Mesopotamian sources and try to discover this aspect of Nebuchadnezzar's reputation.

The Walls of Babylon

Babylon was a city with a long history; evidence so far unearthed suggests that it served as a provincial capital as early as the days of the Third Dynasty of Ur. However, because of the high water table and the huge extent of the settlement, literally nothing is known of what it looked like in the days of Hammurabi and the Kassite kings.[1] Nevertheless, it will be remembered that Nabopolassar, the founder of the Chaldean dynasty, had endeavored to make Babylon the capital of his kingdom.[2] Nearly a century of hostility directed at the city by the Assyrian kings had resulted in much devastation and destruction. Although Esarhaddon (681-669 B.C.) tried to rebuild it in accordance with divine instruction, a revolt during the reign of Aššurbanipal (669-626 B.C.) brought down Assyrian wrath once more. Now, with the end of the seventh century B.C. and the defeat of the Assyrian empire, greater attention could be paid to a restoration of Babylon to its former position of splendor. Nabopolassar, of course, would not live long enough to guide this work to a successful conclusion; Nebuchadnezzar, however, did. His building projects focused not only on the construction of a palace and the restoration of the Esagila but also on the creation of what Babylon perhaps needed most—a series of massive fortification walls.

Excavations by R. Koldewey and his successors have revealed remains of no less than five walls, with three comprising an outer ring and two an inner rampart. They were built of both sun-dried and baked bricks and were of varying degrees of thickness. "Astride the inner wall at regular intervals were projecting towers; similar towers must have protected the outer enceinte also, but no trace of these survives.   The space between the walls was filled with rubble presumably as a base for a protected roadway of sufficient width to permit Herodotus's 'four horse chariot to turn round.'"[3]   Names were associated with both sets of fortifications; the *Imgur-Enlil* and the *Nimitti-Enlil* were designations for the inner and outer walls, respectively.   An unfilled space existed between the walls, and a path served to separate the outer fortification from the moat, so that, as Nebuchadnezzar himself says:

> . . .no pillaging robber might enter into this water sewer, with bright iron bars I closed the entrance to the river, in gratings of iron I set it and fastened it with hinges.   The defences of Esagila and Babylon I strengthened and secured for my reign an enduring name.[4]

The result of all this construction was a city completely surrounded by water and characterized by walls with towers and gates that transformed the largest part of Babylon into "a triangular fortified island. . .elaborately defended and containing the old town with the royal palace, the temple of Marduk and a considerable residential area."[5]   In his own inscriptions, Nebuchadnezzar stresses the significance of this endeavor.   To him, as the servant of Marduk, eternal fame rested on his creation of a rampart that would protect both his citizens and his god's temple from attack:

> In order to strengthen the defenses of Esagila that the evil and the wicked might not oppress Babylon, that which no king had done before me, at the outskirts of Babylon to the east I put about a great wall.   Its moat I dug and its inner moat-wall with mortar and brick I raised mountain-high.   About the sides of Babylon great banks of earth I heaped up.   Great floods of destroying waters like the great waves of the sea I made to flow about it; with marsh I surrounded it.[6]

In placing emphasis on the building of these fortifications, Nebuchadnezzar was no different than the Sumerian hero Gilgamesh, whose rampart enclosing his city of Uruk and whose exploits in the "Land of the Living" entitled him to fashion a stela recording these achievements for all time.   Gilgamesh, in fact, also boasted that he had "raised up the names of the gods" in a manner not seen before his time.

Similar flowery expressions were common in both Nebuchadnezzar's inscriptions[7] and those of the other Chaldean kings. Virtually all Mesopotamian rulers from whom we have records considered defense of their capitals and the maintenance of their god's temples to be the keys to eternal fame. What is interesting is that writers representing other totally different value systems felt exactly the same way. One of the primary focuses of this inquiry is the preoccupation with important achievements such as those associated with Nebuchadnezzar in the writings of the later Greek and Latin authors. The commentators of the classical and Hellenistic periods also sought to stress the importance of a monument of imposing size that had an enduring or lasting quality. In the case of Babylon, they found such a monument in Nebuchadnezzar's own walls.

From Herodotus to Diodorus – A "Classical" View of Babylon

Wiseman has recently pointed out that Nebuchadnezzar, unlike the earlier Assyrian kings, did not have a true capital city or even a royal residence. This was partly the result of an inability of earlier sheiks to bring numerous Aramaean tribes of southern Mesopotamia together. Nebuchadnezzar, however, appears to have been more successful in controlling these tribes than his predecessors, and this success made possible the building of a metropolis that deserved to be called a "wonder" by both the Chaldeans and subject peoples alike. Nebuchadnezzar's royal inscriptions repeatedly describe Babylon as a "great" city, but this adjective did not denote something of incredible size.[8] In this respect, the Chaldean attitude was a mirror-image of the earlier Assyrians, whose cities of Nineveh and Aššur were referred to in the same way. To both the Chaldeans and the Assyrians, the building of administrative or religious capitals for their kingdoms was a commonplace occurrence, the natural result of victorious military campaigns that represented the power and supremacy of their individual gods. The finished product was, then, the symbol of administrative unity and the location of a "palace as the seat of my royal authority, a building for the admiration of my people, a place of union for the land."[9] The victories of Nebuchadnezzar made all of this possible, and the Babylonian priest Berossus, writing three centuries later and reflecting what must have been contained in the complete cuneiform Babylonian chronicles, gives proper credit to the Chaldean king for his achievements:

Nabouchodonosoros learned of his father's death shortly thereafter. After he arranged affairs in Egypt and the remaining territory, he ordered some of his friends to bring the Jewish, Phoenician, Syrian, and Egyptian prisoners together with the bulk of the army and the rest of the booty to Babylonia. He himself set out with a few companions and reached Babylon by crossing the desert. On finding that affairs were being managed by the Chaldeans and the kingship being maintained by the noblest one of these, he took charge of the whole of his father's realm. When the prisoners arrived, he ordered that dwelling places be assigned to them in the most suitable parts of Babylonia. He generously adorned the temple of Bel and the other temples from the war-booty. He strengthened the old city and added the new outer city. He arranged it so that besiegers would no longer be able to divert the river against the city by surrounding the inner city with three circuits of walls and the outer city with three also. The walls of the inner city were made of baked brick and bitumen and those of the outer city of brick alone.[10]

This "local" attitude toward a builder and his accomplishments differs dramatically from what we find in the works of the classical authors, the foremost of whom was, of course, Herodotus. It should not be surprising to find that he set the tone for most of the Greek writers after him. Although there is still some disagreement among scholars as to whether he actually visited Babylon, there can be no question that he believed the city was worthy of more than just a casual mention. It was, indeed, a center of power and authority (as Nebuchadnezzar had envisioned it) with whom the Athenian of his day could readily identify, and any characterization of it had to incorporate the elements of imposing size and almost superhuman power that would set it apart from anything else. Book One of his *Histories* includes this description:

The wall is brought right down to the water on both sides, and at an angle to it there is another wall on each bank, built of baked bricks without mortar, running through the town. There are a great many houses of three and four stories. The main streets and the side streets which lead to the river are all dead straight, and for every one of the side streets or alleys there was a bronze gate in the river wall by which the water could be reached.

The great wall I have described is, so to speak, the breastplate or chief defense of the city; but there is a second one within it, not so thick but hardly less strong. There is a fortress in the middle of each half of the city:

in one the royal palace surrounded by a wall of great strength, in the other the temple of Bel, the Babylonian Zeus.[11]

Although Herodotus was a mere century and a half removed from early Chaldean times, Nebuchadnezzar's name, strangely enough, does not occur in this account. Instead, these marvelous achievements are credited to two queens, Semiramis and Nitocris, with the former being the historic Sammurammat, wife of the Assyrian king Shamshi-Adad V (823-810 B.C.).[12] One of the functions of history (at least to the Greeks of the fifth century B.C.) was to tell a good story. Add to it the element of the "internal" or "long lasting," and the result was a narrative stressing the creation of a metropolitan center that had no equal anywhere. Thus both the city and its creator were in the realm of the "unreal" or the "romantic," possessing qualities that somehow transcended human characteristics. As Herodotus writes:

There have been many kings of Babylon who helped to fortify the city and adorn its temples, and I will tell their story in my History of Assyria. There were also two queens, the earlier, Semiramis, preceding the later by five generations. It was Semiramis who was responsible for certain remarkable embankments in the plain outside the city, built to control the river which until then used to flood the whole countryside. The later of the two queens, Nitocris, was a woman of greater intelligence than Semiramis, and not only left as a memorial of her reign the works which I will presently describe, but also, having her eye on the great and expanding power of the Medes and the many cities, including Nineveh itself, which had fallen before them, took every possible measure to increase her security. For instance, she changed the course of the Euphrates, which flows through Babylon. Its course was originally straight, but by cutting channels higher upstream she made it wind about with so many twists and turns that now it actually passes a certain Assyrian village called Ardericca three separate times, so that anyone today who travels from the Mediterranean to Babylon and comes down the Euphrates finds himself three times over at Ardericcan, on three different days. In addition to this she constructed embankments on both sides of the river of remarkable strength and height, and a long way above the city, close beside the river, dug a basin for a lake some forty-seven miles in circumference. The depth of the basin was governed by the point at which the workmen came to water as they dug down. The soil from the excavation was used for the embankments. When the basin was finished, the queen had stone brought to the place and built up the edge of it the whole way round. The purpose both of the excavation and of the diversion of the river was to cause the frequent bends to reduce the speed of the current, and to prevent a direct voyage downstream to the city. A boat would be faced with a devious course, and at the end of her trip she would have to make the tedious circuit of the lake. Moreover, these works lay in the neighbourhood of the approaches to Assyria and on the direct route to Media, and the intention of the queen was to discourage the Medes from mixing with the people of Babylon and thus getting to know what was going on there. Besides these defenses she was responsible for another undertaking of a less important kind: the city, as I have said, being divided in two by the river, it was necessary under its previous rulers for anyone who wanted to get from one half to the other to cross over by boat and no doubt this was a tiresome business. Nitocris, however, when she was having the basin dug for the lake, had the foresight to make that work a means of getting rid of the inconvenience as well as of leaving yet another monument of her reign. She ordered long stone blocks to be cut, and when they were ready and the excavation complete, she diverted the river into the basin; and while the basin was filling and the original bed of the stream was drying up, she built with burnt brick, on the same pattern as the wall, an embankment on each side of the river where it flowed through the city, and also along the descent to the water's edge from the gates at the end of the side streets; then, as near as possible to the centre of the city, she built a bridge over the river with the blocks of stone which she had had prepared, using iron and lead to bind the blocks together. Between the piers of the bridge she had squared baulks of timber laid down for the inhabitants to cross by—but only during daylight, for every night the timber was removed to prevent people from going over in the dark and robbing each other. Finally when the basin had been filled and the bridge finished, the river was brought back into its original bed, with the result that the basin had been made to serve the queen's purpose, and the people of the town had their bridge into the bargain.[13]

Between the fifth and first centuries B.C., these images of Semiramis and Nitocris were reshaped considerably. This was at least partly the result of the conquest of the Persian empire by Alexander the Great. Herodotus used anti-Persian sources in the writing of his account. "She was said to have executed extensive building programs, including the construction of temples and the enlargement of the irrigation system; but she was not remembered for any martial prowess."[14] Thus although Herodotus's account of the deeds of Semiramis and Nitocris placed no emphasis on conquest, the later descriptions had to emphasize the (re)building of Babylon as the *result* of victorious campaigns. "Within two generations of Herodotus' visit to Mesopotamia, the Babylonians provided themselves with a new mythical history of Semiramis, in which her Assyrians and Babylonians were all-conquering and victorious like the Persians."[15] This so-called second version of the Semiramis legend (identified with the fourth century historian Ktesias) not only attributed divine birth to her, but also represented her as having married the Assyrian king Ninus and as the leader of a military campaign into India where she suffered defeat and was forced to return home. Thus her exploits were similar to those of the Persian kings Cyrus and Darius, the founders and/or great organizers of that empire.

By the time we reach the first century B.C., we find yet another revision of the Semiramis legend in the *Universal History* of Diodorus of Sicily. Although Diodorus had access to a number of sources (Ktesias included) when preparing his account, the achievements of Alexander the Great provided the basis for his characterization.[16] Not only do actual historical events parallel those in the life of Semiramis, but the stress on eternal fame that so deeply permeates the sources for Alexander becomes evident in the description of Semiramis's achievements. This can best be seen in Diodorus's account of her building of Babylon. In it Berossus and the historic Nebuchadnezzar are ignored again, and the "mythical" once more appears in Nebuchadnezzar's place.

Semiramis, whose nature made her eager for great exploits and ambitious to surpass the fame of her predecessor on the throne, set her mind upon founding a city in Babylonia, and after securing the architects of all the world and skilled artisans and making all the other necessary preparations, she gathered together from her entire kingdom two million men to complete the work. Taking the Euphrates river into the centre she threw about the city a wall with great towers set at frequent intervals, the wall being three hundred and sixty stades in circumference, as Ctesias of Cnidus says, but according to the account of Cleitarchus and certain of those who at a later time crossed into Asia with Alexander, three hundred and sixty-five stades; and these later add that it was her desire to make the number of stades the same as the days in the year. Making baked bricks fast in bitumen she built a wall with a height, as Ctesias says, of fifty fathoms, but, as some later writers have recorded, of fifty cubits, and wide enough for more than two chariots abreast to drive upon; and the towers numbered two hundred and fifty, their height and width corresponding to the massive scale of the wall. Now it need occasion no wonder that, considering the great length of the circuit wall, Semiramis constructed a small number of towers; for since over a long distance the city was surrounded by swamps, she decided not to build towers along that space, the swamps offering a sufficient natural defense.

And all along between the dwellings and the walls a road was left two plethra wide.

In order to expedite the building of these constructions she apportioned a stade to each of her friends, furnishing sufficient material for their task and directing them to complete their work within a year. And when they had finished these assignments with great speed she gratefully accepted their zeal, but she took for herself the construction of a bridge five stades long at the narrowest point of the river, skillfully sinking the piers, which stood twelve feet apart, into its bed. And the stones, which were set firmly together she bonded with iron clamps, and the joints of the clamps she filled by pouring in lead. Again, before the piers on the side which would receive the current she constructed cutwaters whose sides were rounded to turn off the water and which gradually diminished to the width of the pier, in order that the sharp points of the cutwaters might divide the impetus of the stream, while the rounded sides, yielding to its force, might soften the violence of the river. This bridge, then, floored as it was with beams of cedar and cypress and with palm logs of exceptional size and having a width of thirty feet, is considered to have been inferior in technical skill to one of the works of Semiramis. And on each side of the river she built an expensive quay of about the same width as the walls and one hundred and sixty stades long.[17]

Eddy recognized long ago[18] that Diodorus's description of Babylon combines an essentially "local," negative reaction to Alexander in Seleucid times with the old Ktesian account of Semiramis's achievements. The result was "a logical extension of previously established native propaganda brought up to date in order to compare Babylonians favorably"[19] with the Macedonians. Furthermore, although Semiramis was still held to have been the daughter of the Syrian goddess Derceto, who was exposed at birth and attended by doves, she also is said to have entered the realm of the gods after her death. Such an association of a builder with divinity by Hellenic or Hellenistic writers only enhanced Babylon's magnificence (as well as its remoteness). After five centuries, the historic Nebuchadnezzar, the creator of Babylon's walls, had become as remote as the city itself. Thus to satisfy the needs of a different audience, the "human" had to become "divine."

Reconstruction of the Ishtar Gate, Babylon.

The Palaces and Hanging Gardens

What emerges from all of the above is the classical author's fascination with an imposing structure of lasting quality. But although the fortification wall surrounding a city the size of Babylon was noteworthy, other structures also captured the interest of either the classical writer or the scribes of Nebuchadnezzar's time for precisely the same reasons. Among these were the Esagila, Marduk's temple in Babylon, and the king's own palaces. Nebuchadnezzar's own flowery building inscriptions indicate that his activities in these areas were widespread. His father, Nabopolassar, chose Babylon as the capital of his kingdom and ruled from a palace near the famous Ishtar gate. "The choice was probably made on the basis of the long tradition of Babylon as 'the centre of the world'."[20] Nebuchadnezzar at first lived in his father's palace, but he later built a residence of his own to the west of it. Wiseman has already noted that "the kings of Babylonia before Nabopolassar used to build palaces and establish residences wherever they pleased, and stored their possessions in them and piled up their belongings there and only in the New Year Festival came to Babylon to please Marduk."[21] Now that the political situation was much more stable, however, Nebuchadnezzar built the so-called Summer Palace in the part of the city still carrying the name Babil. But the Southern Palace was the most important, not only because of its size but because it was located near the Ishtar gate and the "Processional Way," one of the many streets that were a feature of the inner city. Almost every conceivable material was used in its construction, including cedar, ebony, ivory, gold, silver, bronze and lapis lazuli.[22] "The construction," Wiseman notes, "was magnificent," and "the upper walls were decorated all round with a band of blue enamelled bricks" that further enhanced its appearance.[23] Inside the palace was the king's own private residence which, like the rest of the structure, was elaborate in appearance. At the same time, Nebuchadnezzar did work on a number of the city's canals as well as the Processional Way, or the road on which the images of Marduk and Nabû were taken on the way to the *akitu* house when the New Year's festival was celebrated. "Thus the Processional Way − *Ai-ibur-sabû*, 'May the arrogant not flourish' − a title perhaps denoting its use for victory parades − was made into a raised highway (*sule*). At intervals between the Ishtar Gate and Esagil foundation boxes with inscriptions by Nebuchadnezzar commemorated this work."[24]

The Hanging Gardens
and the Greek View of Nebuchadnezzar

In addition to building the Southern Palace, Nebuchadnezzar tells us that he "formed baked bricks into the like(ness of) a mountain and built a large step-terraced. . . structure as a royal abode for myself high up between the double walls of Babylon."[25] Such a description reminds us of the Hanging Gardens that were remembered as one of the seven wonders of the ancient world. Their location has long been a subject for debate, and recently Wiseman, citing new evidence, has suggested that they may have been associated with Nebuchadnezzar's Northern Palace.[26] Whatever the case, both the palace construction and the royal gardens did not escape the attention of the classical and Hellenistic authors. Herodotus identified the royal gardens with Semiramis, while Berossus, continuing to represent local tradition, gave proper credit to Nebuchadnezzar:

After he had walled the city in notable fashion and adorned its gates in a manner befitting a holy place, he built another palace next to the palace of his father. It would perhaps be tedious to describe the height and richness of this palace. . . . In this palace he built and arranged the so-called hanging garden by setting up high stone terraces which he made appear very similar to mountains planted with all kinds of trees. He did this because his wife[27] who had been raised in Media longed for mountainous surroundings.[28]

These Hanging Gardens were remembered as one of the seven wonders of the ancient world. Diodorus Siculus provides us with an elaborate description of them, while attributing their construction to a "Syrian king," an association reminiscent of Berossus's *Babyloniaca*:

There was also, beside the acropolis, the Hanging Garden, as it is called, which was built, not by Semiramis, but by a later Syrian king to please one of his concubines; for she, they say, being a Persian by race and longing for the meadows of her mountains, asked the king to imitate, through the artifice of a planted garden, the distinctive landscape of Persia. The park extended four plethra on each side, and since the approach to the garden sloped like a hillside and the several parts of the structure rose from one another tier on tier, the appearance of the whole resembled that of a theatre.

When the ascending terraces had been built, there had been constructed beneath them galleries which carried the entire weight of the planted garden and rose little by little one above the other along the approach; and the uppermost gallery, which was fifty cubits high, bore the highest surface of the park, which was made level with the circuit wall of the battlements of the city. Furthermore, the walls, which had been constructed at great expense, were twenty-two feet thick, while the passage-way between each two walls was ten feet wide. The roofs of the galleries were covered over with beams of stone sixteen feet long, inclusive of the overlap, and four feet wide. The roof above these beams had first a layer of reeds laid in great quantities of bitumen, over these two courses of baked brick bonded by cement, and as a third layer a covering of lead, to the end that the moisture from the soil might not penetrate beneath. On all this again earth had been piled to a depth sufficient for the roots of the largest trees; and the ground, when levelled off, was thickly planted with trees of every kind that, by their great size or any other charm, could give pleasure to the beholder. And since the galleries, each projecting beyond another, all received the light, they contained many royal lodgings of every description; and there was one gallery which contained openings leading from the top most surface and machines for supplying the garden with water, the machines raising the water in great abundance from the river, although no one outside could see it being done. Now this part, as I have said, was a later construction.[29]

Other Building Activities —
Temples and the Ziqqurat of Babylon

No building program would have been considered complete without the rebuilding or refurbishing of temples, both in Babylon and elsewhere. In this respect, too, Nebuchadnezzar was not unlike his Assyrian predecessors. Not only did he do construction work on temples in Babylon and in twelve other cities throughout Babylonia, but, in some instances, he served as an archaeologist; "I carefully searched for its old substructure,"[30] he repeatedly remarks when recounting details of a shrine's restoration. But the most extensive efforts in this regard were reserved for the Esagila and the Ezida. "I plated the furnishings of Esagil with red gold," he writes,[31] "and the processional boat with yellow gold and (precious) stones (so that it was studded) like the heavens with stars."[32] In like manner, Nebuchadnezzar "completed the work on Ezida and decorated (it) with platings of silver (and) gold and studdings of precious stones." As to the image of Marduk in Esagila he "placed (various stones on the top of his crown, (with other stones) I studded his crown."[33] In all these instances, the emphasis rests on the king's serving as the provider of the gods, and the statement "Nebuchadnezzar indeed provides for our sanctuaries"[34] turns up in many of his inscriptions.

Unfortunately for us, the modern archaeologist has had considerably less luck unearthing remnants of this temple building than he has had with the fortification walls. Koldewey's work at the turn of the century turned up relatively little, because of the depth of the remains. The same is true of the famous staged tower, or *ziqqurat*, located north of the Esagila, that was to become the infamous tower of Babel in the Book of Genesis. Not even a small portion of it remains. Nevertheless, we do know that Nabopolassar had begun to restore it during his reign. "He was to make a new and firmer foundation 'on the heart of the nether world' (i.e., on a sunken platform) and to make its summit rival or equal the heavens."[35] Nebuchadnezzar finished the rebuilding of this Etemenanki ("the structure (that is) the foundation of Heaven and Earth"), even though, as Wiseman notes, the whole project took much time and physical labor to complete:

In undertaking his work on the temple-tower Nebuchadrezzar arranged for the traditional rituals by the *ašipu* exorcists. He claims to have followed the wisdom given by the gods Ea and Marduk to build up the terrace to an overall height of thirty cubits. This was perhaps the height of building remains left by Esarhaddon's partial restoration. Nebuchadrezzar enlarged the temenos to the north and drained it off into the canal to the north and to the gateways of the temple platform. . . . This massive undertaking took many years to complete, as Nebuchadrezzar repeatedly claims it had done. The final work on the filled-in terrace (*tamlu*) and the cladding of the upper dwelling of Marduk with blue-glazed enamelled bricks made the topmost stage look like the heavens themselves. The topping-out was marked by joy and rejoycing.[36]

It is important to note again here that the restoration of temples was a traditional responsibility of Babylonian monarchs. The inscriptions of both Assyrian and Chaldean kings, although quite flowery, treat it as a commonplace occurrence. The classical writer, on the other hand, regarded such monuments as the Esagila and the Etemenanki as something out-of-the ordinary. The Greek mind, in fact, associated temple and palace building with a godlike personage. Herodotus set the tone for what followed when he wrote the following description of Marduk's temple and *ziqqurat* in Babylon:

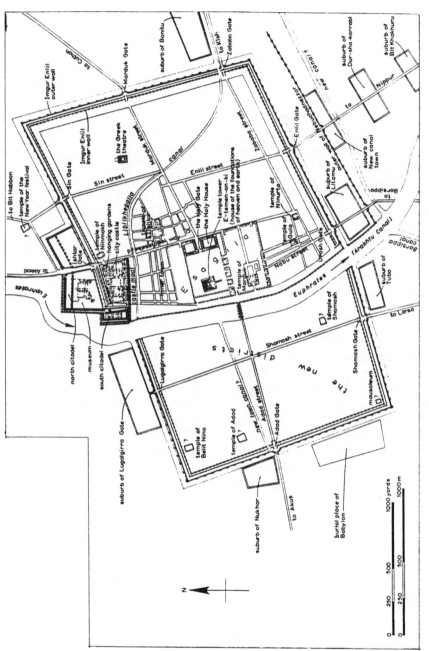

Map of Babylon in the time of Nebuchadnezzar. A reconstruction based on excavations.

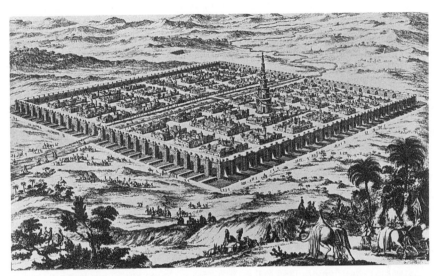

Seventeenth century drawing depicting the city of Babylon as it was thought to have looked in antiquity. From the work of Olfert Dapper (1636-89).

Reconstruction of the outer area of Babylon, mid sixth century, B.C.

The temple is a square building, two furlongs each way, with bronze gates, and was still in existence in my time; it has a solid central tower, one furlong square, with a second erected on top of it and then a third, and so on up to eight. All eight towers can be climbed by a spiral way running round the outside, and about half way up there are seats for those who make ascent to rest on. On the summit of the top most tower stands a great temple with a fine large couch in it, richly covered, and a golden table beside it. The shrine contains no image, and no one spends the night there except (if we may believe the Chaldeans who are the priests of Bel) one Assyrian woman, all alone, whoever it may be that the god has chosen.[37]

Although Herodotus clearly implies that he visited the site, it is unlikely that he did. Diodorus, too, never saw it, but with his description of the temple tower we again enter the realm of the fantastic, with the divine Semiramis given credit for its construction.

After this she built in the centre of the city a temple of Zeus, whom, as we have said, the Babylonians call Belus. Now since with regard to this temple the historians are at variance, and since time has caused the structure to fall in ruins, it is impossible to give the exact facts concerning it. But all agree that it was exceedingly high, and that in it the Chaldeans made their observations of the stars, whose risings and settings could be accurately observed by reason of the height of the structure. Now the entire building was ingeniously constructed at great expense of bitumen and brick, and at the top of the ascent Semiramis set up three statues of hammered gold, of Zeus, Hera, and Rhea. Of these statues that of Zeus represented him erect and striding forward, and, being forty feet high, weighed a thousand Babylonian talents; that of Rhea showed her seated on a golden throne and was of the same weight as that of Zeus; and at her knees stood two lions, while nearby were huge serpents of silver, each one weighting thirty talents. The statue of Hera was also standing, weighing eight hundred talents, and in her right hand she held a snake by the head and in her left a sceptre studded with precious stones. A table for all three statues, made of hammered gold, stood before them, forty feet long, fifteen wide, and weighing five hundred talents. Upon it rested two drinking-cups, weighing thirty talents. And there were censers as well, also two in number but weighing each three hundred talents, and also three gold mixing bowls, of which the one belonging to Zeus weighed twelve hundred Babylonian talents and the other two six hundred each. But all these were later carried off as spoil by the kings of the Persians, while as for the palaces and the other buildings, time has either entirely effaced them or left them in ruins; and in fact of Babylon itself but a small part is inhabited at this time, and most of the area within its walls is given over to agriculture.[38]

Thus from these accounts it would appear that very little escaped the classical writer's attention. Nebuchadnezzar, like Gilgamesh in another time, left behind in Babylon lasting memorials to his god and to his reign that were to ensure his eternal fame in the Mesopotamian sources. The classical author drew upon this body of evidence and, in abstract fashion, perpetuated knowledge of the Chaldean king's achievements in a context that would appeal to his audience. In the process, Herodotus, Berossus, Diodorus, Strabo, and others preserved memory of the city of Babylon through associating it with a number of somewhat superhuman achievements.

The City of Babylon and Nabonidus

It would seem, on the surface at least, that after these building projects of Nebuchadnezzar were concluded successfully, they would have necessitated little in the way of further construction by his successors. By 562 B.C., Babylon was heavily fortified; elaborate palaces housing the royal family were in evidence, and Marduk's temple, the Esagila, stood once more as a symbol of the god's power and the Chaldean king's greatness. However, only seven years after Nebuchadnezzar's death, a series of strange events occurred. Nabonidus, the last king of the dynasty, bore no relation to the royal line. Although he tells us in his own inscriptions that he considered himself to be a legitimate successor of Nebuchadnezzar and Neriglissar, the fact remains that his origins are still unknown, and they clearly represented a source of friction that would eventually result in Persian conquest.[39] Nevertheless, like his predecessors, Nabonidus channeled great energy into the rebuilding of temples in cities throughout his realm. His inscriptions abound with details of excavation and temple building that have few parallels in the records of other earlier Mesopotamian monarchs. The Esagila in Babylon required and received appropriate attention. So did the temple of Shamash in Sippar, and one of our cuneiform texts details his rebuilding of the Ebabbara, which had fallen into ruins:

The inscription of Naram-Sin, son of Sargon (of Akkad), I discovered but did not alter. Anointing it with oil and making sacrifices, I deposited it with my inscriptions and thus returned it to its proper place.

Ebabbar, the temple of the god Shamash, which had long ago become dilapidated and become like a hill of ruins. . .In the reign of Nebuchadnezzar II, a former king, son of Nabopolassar, the sand and mounds of dust which had accumulated on the city and that temple were removed and Nebuchadnezzar discovered the foundation of Ebabbar from the time of Burnaburiash, a former ancient king, but he did not discover the foundation of an older king who preceded Burnaburiash although he looked for it. So he rebuilt Ebabbar on the foundation of Burnaburiash. Then Shamash. . .commanded me, Nabonidus . . . to restore Ebabbar. . .the sand which had covered the city and that temple was taken away. . .its foundation appeared and its layout was exposed. I found therein the inscription of Hammurapi, an old king who seven hundred years before Burnaburiash had built Ebabbar and the temple-tower upon an old foundation for Shamash. I was overcome with awe.

He (the god) showed Nabonidus, his reverent servant who looks after his shrines, the foundation of Naram-Sin, son of Sargon(of Akkad). In that year, in a favourable month, on a propitious day, without altering it one finger-length, Nabonidus laid its base on the foundation of Naram-Sin, son of Sargon—the foundation of Ebabbar, temple of Shamash. He discovered the inscription of Naram-Sin and, without altering it, restored it to its proper place. He deposited it with his own inscriptions. He also discovered inside that old foundation a statue of Sargon, father of Naram-Sin. Half of the head was missing, crumbled, so that one could not discern his face. On account of his reverence for the gods and respect for sovereignty, he brought expert craftsmen and had the head of that statue restored and its face reformed. He did not alter its position. He left it inside Ebabbar and presented an oblation for it.[40]

Yet of overriding concern were the sanctuaries of Sin, the god of the moon worshipped in both Sumerian times and as a primary deity of the Aramu, or northern Aramaeans. In the third millennium B.C., the city of Ur was not only a cult center of Sin, but it was also the capital of the Third Ur Dynasty. Thus we should not be surprised to see Nabonidus attempting to rebuild his temple, even to the extent of tracing its original foundations. His own account of the work reads as follows:

Nabonidus, king of Babylon, patron of the temples Esagil and Ezida, worshipper of the great gods, I: Elugalgalgasisa, the temple-tower of the temple Egishnugal in the city Ur, which the ancient king Ur-Nammu had built but not completed so that his son Shulgi had to complete the work; I examined the inscriptions of Ur-Nammu and his son Shulgi and realized that Ur-Nammu had built but not completed that temple-tower so that his son Shulgi had to complete the work; now that temple-tower had become old. Using as a base the old foundation which Ur-Nammu and his son Shulgi had built, I repaired the damage to that temple-tower, as in olden days, with bitumen and baked brick. For the god Sin, lord of the gods of heaven and underworld, king of the gods, god of the gods who dwell in the highest heaven, lord of Egishnugal in the city Ur, my lord, I rebuilt it.

O Sin, lord of the gods, king of the gods of heaven and underworld, god of the gods who dwell in the highest heaven, when you joyfully enter that temple may there be on your lips blessings for Esagil, Ezida, and Egishnugal, the temples of your great divinity. Reverence for your great divinity instill in my people that they might not sin against your great divinity. May their foundations be as firm as those of heaven. Deliver me, Nabonidus, king of Babylon, from sinning against your great divinity and grant me long life. In Belshazzar, my own offspring, my eldest son, instill reverence for your great divinity that he might have no sin and enjoy an abundant life.[41]

His preoccupation with this god was explained both by Nabonidus himself and by his mother, Adad-guppi—a votaress of Sin in the Syrian city of Harran. In her "autobiography," she not only tells the story of the restoration of Sin's temple, the Ehulhul, but also associates this act with the rise of Nabonidus to power in Babylon:

(Eventually) his wrathful heart quieted down and he became reconciled with the temple Ehulhul, the temple of Sin in Harran, the divine residence in which his heart rejoices, and he had a change of heart. Sin, the king of all the gods, looked with favor upon me and called Nabonidus, my only son, whom I bore, to kingship and entrusted him with the kingship of Sumer and Akkad, (also of) all the countries from the border of Egypt, on the Upper Sea, to the Lower Sea. Then I lifted my hands to Sin, the king of all the gods [I asked] reverently and in a pious mood: (ii) "Since you have called to kingship [Nabonidus, my son, whom I bore, the beloved of his mother,] and have elevated his status, let all the other gods—upon your great divine command—help him (and) make him defeat his enemies, do (also) bring to completion the (re)building of the temple Ehulhul and the performance of its ritual!" In a dream Sin, the king of all the gods, put his hands on me saying: "The gods will return on account of you! I will entrust your son, Nabonidus, with the divine residence of Harran; he will (re)build the temple Ehulhul and complete this task. He will restore and make Harran more (beautiful) than it was before! He will lead Sin, Ningal, Nusku and Sadarnunna in solemn procession into the temple Ehulhul!"

I heeded the words which Sin, the king of all the gods, had spoken to me and saw (them come true). Nabonidus, the only son whom I bore, performed indeed all the forgotten rites of Sin, Ningal, Nusku and Sadarnunna, he completed the rebuilding of the temple Ehulhul, led Sin, Ningal, Nusku and Sadarnunna in procession from Babylon (*Shuanna*), his royal city, installed (them again) in gladness and happiness into Harran, the seat which pleases them.[42]

The Persians capitalized on this fascination with Sin to propagandize Nabonidus's lack of devotion to Marduk. And therein probably lies the reason for much of the "negative press" given the city of Babylon in the Old Testament and the *Midrash Rabbah*. To the Persians (who conquered it) and the Greek historians of classical times, the city symbolized both power and permanence. The Hebrews, however, had experienced first hand both the construction projects of Nebuchadnezzar and the "heresy" of Nabonidus. To them, Babylon stood for something quite different. Stories about it had to serve a didactic purpose, while keeping alive the memory of fifty years of captivity. The Book of Daniel became the repository of most of these tales,[43] and the information contained in them would create the only negative image of "Nebuchadnezzar the builder" in the whole of ancient source material. To the Hebrews, historicity in this context was of only minimal importance; instead, what was significant was the mythical figure emerging as a result of a combination of history and fiction. Thus although the foregoing accounts of Nabonidus's achievements were well known after the Babylonian Captivity ended, they were to contribute greatly to the "Myth of Nebuchadnezzar," as we shall see.

6

The "Myth" of Nebuchadnezzar

But it seems that the people of Jerusalem call everybody who destroyed their town Nebuchadnezzar.

—Al Biruni

Having enumerated the sources for the reigns of Nebuchadnezzar (and Nabonidus), we now must evaluate their contents. Such an evaluation can only be accomplished when considering their broader cultural context. Each individual clearly meant different things to different people; the memory of each king was preserved by various chroniclers, historians, or biographers for altogether dissimilar purposes. To the Greeks, Nabonidus was nothing more than a name in a list, but to the Persians his reign stood out as an example never to be repeated again.[1] Because such diverse descriptions exist in the documents, it stands to reason that a multiplicity of folkloristic elements can be associated with each one, elements that not only enhance the picture of the individual being described, but also preserve a cultural attitude toward such a person in accordance with his peculiar achievements. In the following pages, an attempt is made to analyze these elements as they were applied throughout the centuries to Nebuchadnezzar.

Nebuchadnezzar in the Greek and Latin Sources

The descriptions of the Chaldean period that are preserved in the classical sources are, understandably, the most difficult to analyze. There are many reasons for this. First, most of the information that has survived is found in the works of chroniclers such as Julius Africanus and Eusebius; as we have noted, these chroniclers did not see the "biographizing" of history as their responsibility; instead their task was to treat in comparative fashion the histories of all known civilizations in the process of dealing with the evolution of human existence from the creation of the world to their own time.[2] Unfortunately, the comments contained in these documents are brief.

Second, with the exception of the writings of Berossus and Josephus, no other source beyond the chronicles preserves these valuable descriptions. Therefore it is virtually impossible to determine the *nature* of the work that originally contained these accounts. Without knowing the original objectives of these early writers, we cannot easily determine what each author considered particularly important to each characterization. Finally, while the *Histories* of Herodotus, the *Universal History* of Diodorus Siculus, or the *Geography* of Strabo are largely preserved in their original form, they treat historical figures in a very abstract manner; the result is a "mythologizing" of the character, sometimes ignoring the name of the individual altogether while conjuring up an image that can be connected with several real persons.[3] Nevertheless, despite these obstacles it is worthwhile to attempt an analysis of what survives, because enough is available to create at least an image of what the classical author thought important enough to preserve in a figure.

It should be obvious to even casual observers that the Greek mind idolized the monumental. Any famous metropolis that could not be visited easily by a "man on the street" was a topic of great interest and was incorporated as a noteworthy feature into the historian's work.[4] Thus not surprisingly Babylon fascinated nearly everyone. Its imposing walls and *ziqqurat* were, like the so-called Cyclopaean walls of Mycenae,[5] literally "unreal." Because the creation itself was extraordinary, the creator(s) had to be equally extraordinary. Thus Diodorus Siculus and Strabo confused historical truth by not only combining the achievements of several kings into one image but also by collecting the features of several ancient urban centers and creating, in reality, one giant metropolis built by one or two "superfigures." Babylon and Nineveh became one city built by two Assyrian queens with hellenized names; one of them, Semiramis, even seemed to be god-like.[6] The "universal" histories, written between ca. 450 B.C. and A.D. 50 by people who may not have visited the areas they described, abstracted historical figures and created a nearly universal image of a builder. They portray actual human achievements in the context of a superhuman, with actual historical names of only secondary concern or consideration.

Only when we look at the histories written by men whose scope narrowed considerably does the abstract give place to the concrete; local tradition and historical fact are more evident, and names come to have meaning. This can be seen first in Megasthenes, a native of the area whose history he describes. This Seleucid official had access to records pertaining to the neo-Babylonian period. In the fragment of his work preserved by Abydenus, we are told

That Nabucodrosorus (Nebuchadnezzar), having become more powerful than Hercules, invaded Libya and Iberia, . . .and when he had rendered them tributary, he extended his conquests over the inhabitants of the shores upon the right of the sea.[7]

It is obvious from this statement that Megasthenes, like other Greek writers commenting on different periods, considered these achievements to be somehow in the realm of the superhuman. However, his characterization of Nebuchadnezzar as a builder provides further evidence of the Hellenic fascination with such magnificent accomplishments. He writes:

It is said that from the beginning all things were water, called the sea [Thalath]; that Belus caused this state of things to cease, and appointed to each its proper place, and he [Belus] surrounded Babylon with a wall; but in process of time this wall disappeared, and Nabuchodonosor [Nebuchadnezzar] walled it in again, and it remained so, with its brazen gates, until the time of the Macedonian conquest, [i.e., by Alexander the Great], and after other things he says: Nabuchodonosor having succeeded to the kingdom, built the walls of Babylon in a triple circuit in fifteen days; and he turned the river Armacale, a branch of the Euphrates and the Acracanus; and above the city of Sippara he dug a receptacle for the waters, whose perimeter was forty parasangs, and whose depth was twenty cubits; and he placed gates at the entrance thereof.[8]

Two items in this segment are noteworthy. First, Nebuchadnezzar is said to have completed the triple circuit wall in just fifteen days, which clearly places the achievement in the realm of the marvelous. Second, Megasthenes clearly relates Nebuchadnezzar's reign to the time of Belus, the founder of Babylon who was viewed as a god by Hellenic writers. No other king, either Babylonian or Assyrian, is mentioned as having anything to do with such work. Although Nebuchadnezzar is not referred to as a god-king, it is clear what Megasthenes had in mind. Belus, to the Hellenistic world, was considered the first king in Mesopotamia after the creation.[9] The city that he founded (and its walls) was truly a wonder of the ancient world. The creator of such a wonder was worthy of "immortalization" through preservation of an account of his achievements, and what better way could there be of keeping alive such a memory than to speak to Nebuchadnezzar's Babylon in the context of Belus's original wall? Unfortunately, more of Megasthenes's *History of India* does not survive to provide us with an even more complete picture of Nebuchadnezzar from a Seleucid point of view combining a Hellenic characterization of a Chaldean king with historical fact.

This account would have very little meaning had not similar descriptions existed in sources that are roughly contemporary. Such a contemporary account exists in the *Babyloniaca* of Berossus. Although this work also survives only in fragments, it is quoted by several chronographers[10] and gives evidence that the author actually consulted works preserved in the temple of Marduk in Babylon. When speaking of Nebuchadnezzar, Berossus describes not only his conquest of Syria and Egypt, but also relates the story of the conquest of Jerusalem and the deportation of the Hebrews.[11] However, his most lengthy description is that of Babylon and its massive walls. When discussing Nebuchadnezzar's accomplishments, he includes the following:

> He also rebuilt the old city, (Babylon), and added another to it on the outside, and so far restored Babylon, that none who should besiege it afterwards might have it in their power to divert the river, so as to facilitate an entrance into it; and this he did by building three walls around the inner city, and three about the outer one. Some of these walls he built of burnt brick, and bitumen, and some of brick only. When he had thus admirably fortified the city with walls, and had magnificently adorned the gates, he added also a new palace to those in which his forefathers had dwelt, adjoining them, but exceeding them in height and in its great splendour. It would, perhaps, require too long a narration, if any one were to describe it; however as prodigiously large and magnificent as it was, it was finished in fifteen days. In this palace he erected very high walks, supported by stone pillars; and by planting what was called a pensile paradise, and replenishing it with all sorts of trees, he rendered the prospect an exact resemblance of a mountainous country. This he did to please his queen, because she had been brought up in Media, and was fond of a mountainous situation.[12]

This account corresponds most closely to the contents of Nebuchadnezzar's own inscriptions and to archaeological evidence unearthed since 1899 at Babylon. It also is quite similar to the version given by Megasthenes[13] and gives us further indications of the emphasis placed on such enduring accomplishments by Hellenic authors. Obviously, Berossus could either read cuneiform writing himself or had someone readily available who could read it for him. The questions arise about the audience for which these works were intended and about peculiar folkloristic elements, common to such writings, which tended to categorize certain historical individuals. Because of the fragmentary condition of these sources, it is difficult to ascertain their exact nature or to determine the extent of the information provided for each individual in the original source.[14] However, although the conquests of Nebuchadnezzar are also noted, the *primary* emphasis is on that which appeared to be "out-of-the-ordinary." The city of Babylon was singled out for its imposing size, its enduring quality, and its creation within a remarkably short period of time. Both Berossus and Megasthenes composed their works in the Seleucid period with first-hand knowledge of the monuments and of Nebuchadnezzar. But it is possible that they were writing exclusively for a *Seleucid* audience, a "local" Greek public which could identify itself *geographically* with the times and people these men were writing about. The *Histories* of Herodotus and the volumes of Diodorus Siculus, although written earlier, were universal in scope. Their audience was not conditioned by location or by time; everyone throughout the Greek or Roman world had to be reached by "universalizing" the characters described.[15] The same emphasis on the unusual appears in Strabo and others; the farther removed the audience is *geographically* from the setting of the story, the more marvelous it must become. Hence these men tended to almost deify their subjects, emphasizing qualities considered unusual in the realm of human achievement. In the *oikumene* the "monumental" was noteworthy as an accomplishment that was somehow superhuman in its character. The audience of that *oikumene* understood these things if they were linked to a god-like being and universalized. For the local Seleucid audience, Berossus and Megasthenes needed only to relate historical fact to a tradition linking such achievements to the *will* of a god. Marduk gave Nebuchadnezzar the abilities to restore Babylon and build its walls; thus the Belus of Berossus and Megasthenes was linked to the king to suggest indirectly that a divine desire determined Nebuchadnezzar's accomplishments. It is important, therefore, to remember that the unusual was a part of the "lore" of the Greek historians; however, a description of the unusual varied in accordance with the *nature* of the audience addressed.[16]

The Achaemenids and Nabonidus

What seemed awe-inspiring or unusual to the Greeks did not necessarily mean the same thing to people of other cultures. Such was the case with the Achaemenids.[17]   The Persians, after all, were builders, too; the Persepolis of Darius the Great may not have been an administrative or military capital, yet it was a showplace to which subject peoples brought their annual tribute.   Hence the building projects of Nebuchadnezzar, although important and impressive, were not necessarily out of the ordinary; nor were the restorations of sanctuaries that were characteristic of the reign of Nabonidus, because this also was considered a traditional responsibility of Babylonian kings.   Instead, the unusual amounted to an action or behavior that went *contrary* to the traditional will of a god.   Cyrus II, of course, had to cast his own image in a favorable light; having taken Babylon through force and betrayal, it was necessary to be propagandistic in justifying his success.[18]   These circumstances led to the creation by the priest-scribe of Marduk in Babylon of an account that focused on the outright "heretical" acts of the last king of the Chaldean period. Nebuchadnezzar's 43-year reign was one in which devotion to Marduk was accepted fact; Nabonidus, on the other hand, not only halted the New Year's festival but also forsook his kingdom for a sojourn to Tema.[19]   But the most hated act of all was his preoccupation with the god Sin of Harran (presumably the city of his origin).   The lengthy text detailing the life of Adad-guppi, Nabonidus's mother, tells us of his connection with this god:

> I lifted up my hands and prayed with reverence and piety to Sin, king of the gods: "Nabonidus, my son, the issue of my womb, beloved of his mother, you have appointed to the sovereignty.   You have pronounced his name.   By command of your great divinity may the great gods go at his side and may they conquer his foes.!"[20]

An account like this could never appear in an inscription in Babylon, formulaic though it may be.   Nor could an image of Sin be displayed in the capital city.   Yet the *Verse Account* of Nabonidus emphasized both. Furthermore, the grave consequences of such a deed were noted and attributed to a lack of devotion to Marduk, so that a picture emerged of a king who dwelt away from men[21] and who was largely isolated from civilization as he knew it.   To the Babylonians under Persian rule (and the Jews in the Post Exilic period), then, Nabonidus was, literally, mad, unworthy of the devotion of his subjects. As we will see, many of the characterizations included here are found in other sources where they are used for different reasons.

The Hebrew Sources[22]

Unlike the classical sources, the name of Nabonidus appears in the Hebrew material only in the *Chronicle* of Jerechmeel, but Nebuchadnezzar is virtually everywhere. Why was he so prominently mentioned? Clearly, not for the fortification of Babylon[23]; the reason lies in the conquest of Judah. The capture of the city of Jerusalem, the dismantling of the temple of Solomon, and the deportation of captives were acts never to be forgotten; the author of such horrible deeds had to be portrayed in such a way as not only to emphasize the destruction and wickedness but also to show that the apparent power or might of the king of Babylon was merely the result of Yahweh's punishment of the Hebrews. The king was only a tool to be used in the teaching of a lesson. In this light, a characterization of Nebuchadnezzar had to be richly embellished with elements drawn from a number of sources, folkloristic or otherwise. In the process, however, the Hebrew writer used borrowed historical materials associated with Nabonidus, not because he was "confused" but because Nabonidus appeared in his own and later sources in a way that *fit* the situation involving Nebuchadnezzar that was being described.

Through the years students of the Old Testament and the patristic (as well as the rabbinic) commentaries have concerned themselves with questions relating to the preservation of oral tradition. This becomes particularly evident when examining various opinions concerning the contents of the Book of Daniel.[24] The spectrum here is unbelievably broad; some scholars have tried to literally associate history with the sequence of events described in chapters 2–4; others have denied historicity altogether and dealt with their source only in the light of fairy-tale-like parallels found in the writings of other cultures.[25] Although both approaches have their merits, they fail to consider the purpose for which these stories were intended. Von Soden pointed this out more than four decades ago.[26] Consequently, the material in Daniel 2-4 is often referred to in the context of a confusion of sources, implying that the author did not have a clear idea of what he sought to represent. Close examination will demonstrate that the Hebrew writer *did* indeed have a correct knowledge of history in the Post-Exilic period; he did, however, represent a character as he thought he *should* be represented so as to fulfill the purposes of a didactic treatise. If the end result appeared to a historian or a literary critic as confusion, it was simply the product of a misunderstanding of what the author intended to do. Drawing from folklore and history, his desire was to create a figure whose attributes could be applied to any future individual monarch who dared emulate the architect of the Babylonian Captivity.

The Book of Daniel and the Midrash Rabbah

After briefly outlining the setting of his story, the author of the Book of Daniel proceeds with a description of Nebuchadnezzar and his disturbing dream, the meaning of which is known to Daniel *before* the actual event takes place. By the time we reach chapter 3, the Babylonian monarch is setting up the image that is to be worshipped in the kingdom. Two points are noteworthy here. First, the recording of dreams is a common occurrence in the ancient Near East, particularly in Mesopotamia. Second, while Nebuchadnezzar's dream is being interpreted here, the cuneiform sources show that Nabonidus is preoccupied with dreams more than any other Babylonian or Assyrian king. The contents of this "dream literature" vary in accordance with the places in which the texts were composed; nevertheless, in all of the documents Nabonidus carried out the will of a particular god and repaired the temples of Sin and restored his image. Examples of such dreams follow.

> During my lawful rule, the great Lords became reconciled with this town and (its) temple out of love for my kingship; they had mercy (upon the town) and they let me see a dream in the very first year of my everlasting rule: Marduk, the Great Lord, and Sin, the luminary of heaven and earth, stood (there) both; Marduk said to me: "Nabonidus, king of Babylon, bring bricks on your own chariot (drawn by your own horse, (re) build the temple É.HÚL.HÚL and let Sin, the Great Lord, take up his dwelling there!" I said to the Ellil of the gods, Marduk: "The *Umman-manda* (here for: the Medes) are laying siege to the very temple which you have ordered (me) to (re) build and their armed might is very great!". . .(And indeed) when the third year came to pass, he (Marduk) made rise against them Cyrus, king of Anshan, his young servant, and he (Cyrus) scattered the numerous *Umman-manda* with his small army and captured Astyages, king of the *Umman-manda* and brought him in fetters into his (Cyrus') land. That was the doing of the Great Lord Marduk whose command cannot be changed.[27]

Nabonidus, king of Babylon, patron of the temples Esagil and Ezida, worshipper of the great gods, I: Elugalgalgasisa, the temple-tower of the temple Egishnugal in the city Ur, which the ancient king Ur-Nammu had built but not completed so that his son Shulgi had to complete the work; I examined the inscriptions of Ur-Nammu and his son Shulgi and realized that Ur-Nammu had built but not completed that temple-tower so that his son Shulgi had to complete the work; now that temple-tower had become old. Using as a base the old foundation which Ur-Nammu and his son Shulgi had built, I repaired the damage to that temple-tower, as in olden days, with bitumen and baked brick. For the god Sin, lord of the gods of heaven and underworld, king of the gods, god of the gods who dwell in the highest heaven, lord of Egishnugal in the city Ur, my lord, I rebuilt it.

O Sin, lord of gods, king of the gods of heaven and underworld, god of the gods who dwell in the highest heaven, when you joyfully enter that temple may there be on your lips blessings for Esagil, Ezida, and Egishnugal, the temples of your great divinity. Reverence for your great divinity instill in my people that they might not sin against your great divinity. May their foundations be as firm as those of heaven. Deliver me, Nabonidus, king of Babylon, from sinning against your great divinity and grant me long life. In Belshazzar, my own offspring, my eldest son, instill reverence for your great divinity that he might have no sin and enjoy an abundant life.[28]

These examples are cited to illustrate Nabonidus's devotion to Sin. Although these same documents may not have been the sources from which the Hebrew writer drew his material, something similar to them likely served as the foundation on which the legend of Nebuchadnezzar was built. Certainly, the Achaemenids needed to (and did) emphasize Nabonidus's lack of attention to Marduk; when the Hebrews returned to Palestine, they carried with them their own hatred for Nebuchadnezzar plus the Persian hostility toward Nabonidus and, consequently, merged both into a story of a conqueror-king who forsook his god and required worship of another by his subjects. As we read in Daniel:

Nebuchadnezzar the king made an image of gold, whose height was threescore cubits, and the breadth thereof six cubits: he set it up in the plain of Dura, in the province of Babylon.

Then Nebuchadnezzar the king sent to gather together the princes, the governors, and the captains, the judges, the treasurers, the counsellors, the sheriffs, and all the rulers of the provinces, to come to the dedication of the image which Nebuchadnezzar the king had set up.

Then the princes, the governors, and captains, the judges, the treasurers, the counsellors, the sheriffs, and all the rulers of the provinces, were gathered together unto the dedication of the image that Nebuchadnezzar the king had set up; and they stood before the image that Nebuchadnezzar had set up (Daniel 3:1-3).

An important parallel can be made to the narrative in Genesis (40-1) of Joseph interpreting the dreams of the pharaoh. The "courtly tales" involving Joseph are almost identical with those found in Daniel 2ff. and are characterized by virtually similar motifs inherited from wisdom literature. The two stories have a similar purpose – to magnify the God of Heaven over against the heathen deities, and to paint a negative picture of the pharaoh and Nebuchadnezzar while highlighting the skill and sagacity of the Jewish sage. Compare, for example, the motif of Joseph cast aside in a dungeon with that of Daniel in the lion's den and Ahiqar in prison. All three figures are "scribes" in the diplomatic sense and appear as high administrative figures in their respective contexts.[29]

After this we are presented (chapter 4) with the story of the madness of Nebuchadnezzar. Here folkloristic elements, pure and simple, predominate:

The same hour was the thing fulfilled upon Nebuchadnezzar: and he was driven from men, and did eat grass as oxen, and his body was wet with the dew of heaven, till his hairs were grown like eagles' feathers, and his nails like birds' claws. (4:33)

This passage reflects the contents of the *Lives of the Prophets*[30] and the *Wisdom of Ahiqar* discussed earlier. It describes a prisoner isolated from men long enough so as to change his physical appearance. The prisoner Ahiqar (according to the story, during the reign of Sennacherib, king of Assyria), emerged from the dungeon in a similar state.

And forthwith the king mounted his chariot, and came unto me in haste, and opened (my) prison over me, and I ascended and came and fell before the king; the hair of my head had grown down on my shoulders, and my beard reached my breast; and my body was fouled with the dust, and my nails were grown long like eagles.[31]

This description also echoes the *Prayer of Nabonidus* quoted earlier, in which the king is said to have lived apart from men for seven years.[32] Perhaps herein lies as fine an example as can be found of a melding of history and oral tradition. Nabonidus's own inscriptions inform us of his three-year (at least) absence from Babylon. The *Verse Account of Nabonidus*, although it clearly exaggerates this fact for political reasons, essentially preserves historical fact.[33] The *Prayer of Nabonidus*, written in Aramaic, further emphasizes this point while adding a purely folkloristic description to the picture. The traditional image of a prisoner is thus superimposed on both a historical figure and an essentially factual account of his activities. The Maccabean author(s) of the Book of Daniel, four centuries removed from the Chaldean period, chose to substitute the name of Nebuchadnezzar for that of Nabonidus, not because of an ignorance of history or because the events of the Exilic period were forgotten,[34] but because Nebuchadnezzar was the architect of the Babylonian Captivity, and a didactic commentary could best realize its objectives through a portrayal of a king that combined history and fiction. To the Hebrew writer, it mattered not whether a characterization harmonized with historical accuracy; the events of the reign of Nabonidus could be combined with the destruction of Jerusalem by Nebuchadnezzar to construct an image of a king that could be easily related to the rule of any monarch at any point in time.[35]

No better illustration of this point can be found than in the *Midrash Rabbah*. Although ten of the midrashim specifically mention Nebuchadnezzar's name, most of them can be clearly related to the destruction of the second temple by the armies of the Roman emperors Vespasian and Titus. Not only is the king said to have resided at Daphne to meet with the Sanhedrin[36] and to have "shaken arrows" in the name of Rome, Alexandria, and Jerusalem,[37] but his "legions" suggest to him that the temple in Jerusalem be destroyed. As we read in *Esther Rabbah*:

They are the Decumanian and Augustan legions. It was these which suggested to Nebuchadnezzar that he should go up and destroy the Temple.[38]

This Nebuchadnezzar is described subsequently as having behaved like a beast who tears flesh apart before eating it.[39] Thus, as with the Arabic sources, everyone who besieges Jerusalem is thought of as a Nebuchadnezzar; the characterization of the figure knows no limits of time or space and is applicable to all periods of history.

7

Concluding Remarks

This inquiry proposed to give two separate audiences an idea of what Nebuchadnezzar meant to people who represented several different value systems. Obviously, such a study is not without its difficulties, primarily because of the unevenness of the written record. We have seen that Nebuchadnezzar's own contemporary cuneiform sources are incomplete, despite the fact that his reign was the longest of the Chaldean dynasty. Furthermore, the Greek, Latin, and Hebrew secondary sources are sometimes difficult to interpret, because many of them do not exist in their original form: they are only fragments represented in other works. Nevertheless, what remains enables a number of conclusions to be drawn. In the next few paragraphs I hope to address some of these conclusions and raise one or two broader questions that go beyond the scope of the present investigation.

Nebuchadnezzar's contemporary cuneiform sources, like those of his Assyrian and Chaldean predecessors, stress conquest and devotion to the gods through restoration work and temple building as the keys to eternal fame. After the conquest of the Persian empire by Alexander the Great, this traditional view of a Babylonian monarch was perpetuated in the sources surviving from Seleucid Mesopotamia, despite the fact that some were written in Greek. Writers like Berossus viewed the achievements of a monarch such as Nebuchadnezzar as not having been overshadowed by those of the Macedonians, even though the Persian empire (including Chaldean Mesopotamia) had been conquered by them. Neither Nebuchadnezzar's campaigns into Syria, Phoenicia, and Egypt nor his attempt to make Babylon the "center of the world" through extensive building projects were overlooked. Indeed, an essentially "local" reaction portrayed Nebuchadnezzar in a positive light by stressing the accomplishments of the Babylonian monarch as models for Alexander's successors. Admittedly, the sources surviving Seleucid antiquity are fragmentary or incomplete, but what survives suggests the perpetuation of a tradition among Mesopotamian subjects of the Seleucid kings that varied little from the Chaldeans who preceded them. The "local" view of a monarch in political or propagandistic literature did not die with the conquest of the Persian empire.

On the other hand, classical or Hellenistic authors who were not native to Mesopotamia stressed these same achievements for altogether different purposes. In part, they wanted to tell a good story about places and people not easily visited or recognized by the citizens of Athens or Rome in classical times. However, the tradition of superhuman achievement going back to Homeric times dictated a stress on monuments of enduring character and on the persons responsible for them. The Assyrians and Chaldeans, no less than the Greeks and Romans, were city and temple builders. Their cities and temples were as far removed geographically from the Athens and Rome of Herodotus and Diodorus Siculus as they were chronologically from the Mycenae of Agamemnon or the Sparta of Menelaus. Their creators had to be as extraordinary as the cities themselves, even to the extent of being gods or god-like. Nebuchadnezzar, the builder of Babylon, lost his historical identity to become a totally different figure. This is not to say that the sources used by Herodotus or Diodorus Siculus did not have political overtones. The characterization differed slightly from the fifth to the first century B.C. However, the superhuman element was never totally absent. The farther removed the source is from the true historical setting, the more "unreal" the description becomes. The historical Nebuchadnezzar, beginning as a human being with extraordinary qualities, changes into the child of a goddess who returns to the divine realm after death.

The Heroic Image –
Parallels in Classical and Hellenistic Literature

Illustrations supporting these conclusions abound in classical and Hellenistic sources. They also provide evidence of the relationship of popular tradition or folklore to the development of a characterization. Homer's *Iliad* refers to the Mycenae of Agamemnon and the Troy of Priam as virtually impregnable citadels that symbolized the power of their respective inhabitants. They provided a reason for the classical, Hellenistic, and Roman authors to associate their creation with a race of superhumans, the Cyclopes, whose feats had no parallel anywhere. Pausanias, in the second century A.D., even linked the failure of later attempts to capture Mycenae with its "mythical" builders. As we read in his *Description of Greece*:

Though the Argives could not take the wall of Mycenae by storm, built as it was like the wall of Tiryns by the Cyclopes, as they were called, yet the Mycenaeans were forced to leave their city through lack of provisions.[1]

Toelken's definition of folklore[2] suggests the existence of paradigms into which virtually any heroic or villainous individual fits. Evidence from the writings of Herodotus and Diodorus Siculus supports this view. These paradigms transcend time itself and allow a culture to characterize particular achievements in either a positive or negative light. For example, by the time Herodotus wrote, the Babylon of Nebuchadnezzar was virtually a memory. Yet like the Mycenae of Agamemnon's day, Babylon symbolized power and magnificence. Knowledge of it could best be preserved by portraying it as a city of "enormous size" that surpassed "in splendour any city of the known world."[3] Its creator had to be similarly abstract and associated with numerous "incidents" that suggested god-like qualities. The question of historicity was clearly irrelevant; the classical author, dealing with a historical figure such as Nebuchadnezzar, portrayed a real person who accomplished an unusual deed, such as the building of the walls of Babylon and the diversion of the course of the Euphrates, in such a way as to subordinate fact to the ideal image of a hero. He related to an audience that was conditioned (in the epic tradition identified with Homer) to expect a figure to be either a god or god-like;[4] Nebuchadnezzar had to be identified with either Belus of the creation story or the mythical queen Semiramis as a divine being doing superhuman things. As we read in Diodorus Siculus's *Universal History*:

Semiramis, whose nature made her eager for great exploits and ambitious to surpass the fame of her predecessor on the throne, set her mind upon founding a city in Babylonia, and after securing the architects of all the world and skilled artisans and making all the other necessary preparations, she gathered together from her entire kingdom two million men to complete the work. Taking the Euphrates river into the centre she threw about the city a wall with great towers set at frequent intervals, the wall being three hundred and sixty states in circumference, as Ctesias of Cnidus says, but according to the account of Cleitarchus and certain of those who at a later time crossed into Asia with Alexander, three hundred and sixty-five stades; and these later add that it was her desire to make the number of stades the same as the days in the year. Making baked bricks fast in bitumen she built a wall with a height, as Ctesias says, of fifty fathoms, but, as some later writers have recorded, of fifty cubits, and wide enough for more than two chariots abreast to drive upon; and the towers numbered two hundred and fifty, their height and width corresponding to the massive scale of the wall. Now it need occasion no wonder that, considering the great length of the circuit wall, Semiramis constructed a small number of towers; for since over a long distance the city was surrounded by swamps, she decided not to build towers along that space, the swamps offering a sufficient natural defence. And all along between the dwellings and the walls a road was left two plethra wide.[5]

This treatment of Nebuchadnezzar and his achievements fits a paradigm that was associated (at different times by various writers) with Theseus and other heroic figures as well.

The Villain Motif

However, the building activities and conquests of Nebuchadnezzar did not preclude the possibility of a thoroughly negative characterization. The Hebrews provide a case in point. Although the Athens of Herodotus, the Babylon of Berossus, or the Rome of Diodorus Siculus were unaffected by the campaigns and conquests of Nebuchadnezzar, Judah and its inhabitants definitely were his victims. Reacting to their own history, Herodotus and Berossus portrayed the Persians or the Macedonians in a negative light by comparison with the achievements of Nebuchadnezzar. By contrast, the Hebrews characterized Nebuchadnezzar through a combination of his destruction of the Temple of Solomon and the "heresy" of Nabonidus to produce an image of a conqueror that (like the Greek image of a builder) transcended space and time and served didactic purposes. The conquest of Judah and the taking of Jerusalem had to be avenged. Nebuchadnezzar, in a purely folkloristic way, became a "creature of the fields" who was being punished for what he did; anyone who emulated him would suffer the same fate. The *Chronicle* of Jerachmeel treats the subject in the following way:

LXVI. (1) Nebuchadnezzar was not very much changed in his being from other men; but only in his appearance, in his mind, and in his language. He appeared to men like an ox as far as his navel (or stomach), and from his navel to his feet like a lion. He ate the herbs at first which other men eat, to show that he chewed his food like an ox, and became at last like a lion, in that he killed all the wicked. Many people went out to see him, but Daniel did not, because, during the time of this change, he was praying for him, so that the seven years became seven months. For forty days he roamed about among the wild beasts, and for the next forty days his heart became like that of any other man, and he wept on account of his sins. Again, for forty days he wandered about in caves, and for yet another forty days he roamed among the wild beasts until the seven months were completed.

(2) When, however, the Lord restored him to his former position he no longer reigned alone, but appointed seven judges, one for each year until the expiration of the seven years. And during this time, while he was repenting for his sins, he neither ate meat nor bread, nor drank any wine, but his food consisted of herbs and seed, according to Daniel's counsel.[6]

Examples such as these illustrate the use of aspects of the classical, Hellenistic, and Hebrew value systems in creating images of the historical Nebuchadnezzar that transcended history itself. He became a figure with clearly mythical qualities.

This investigation began with an attempt to find history in Nebuchadnezzar's own cuneiform sources. Later, we found that the Jews of the Hellenistic period, although familiar with the Babylonian Captivity, transformed Chaldean sources into didactic treatises that had no time or space limits. History became mythistory, combining a classical Greek attitude toward a figure with the somewhat apocalyptic view of his deeds found in the *Dynastic Prophecy*. A question, then, that still needs to be addressed is when did this transformation take place? One possibility is that it occurred in Seleucid times, especially given the similarity of attitudes reflected in the Hebrew and Hellenistic sources. The Seleucids (as well as the Chaldeans) used the "prophecy text" for purely political purposes (see chap. 3). Yet what we find in Daniel 2-4 can be construed to have political overtones as well. The possibility exists that the Seleucids exerted an influence that caused a transformation of this genre into one with mainly political overtones. In a time of obvious turbulence, in an age when religious faith might be repeatedly tested, this would seem understandable. Let us hope that the future will provide a more complete understanding of the cultural relationships that may have then existed and influenced the sources that survive today.

Notes

Chapter 1. Introduction

1. For a summary of the events leading to the conquest of Babylon by Cyrus of Persia, see Joan Oates, *Babylon* (London: Thames & Hudson, 1979), 130ff.

2. For an account of the reign of Nebuchadnezzar I, see John A. Brinkman, *A Political History of Post-Kassite Babylonia 1158-722 B.C. (=Analecta Orientalia 43).* (Rome: 1968), 113ff. For an early study of his importance, see William J. Hinke, *A New Boundary Stone of Nebuchadrezzar I, from Nippur (=Babylonian Expedition, Researches,* no. 4) (Philadelphia: 1907), 116ff.

3. For a sketch of the events leading to the establishment of the Chaldean dynasty, see M. Dandamaev, *Slavery in Babylonia,* trans. Victoria Powell (DeKalb: Northern Illinois University Press, 1984), 36ff. A summary of recent literature on the subject also is included. It should be noted that although Dandamaev refers to Chaldeans as Aramaeans, there is no direct evidence in the cuneiform sources to support this. In fact, the Hellenistic writers used the terms Chaldeans and Babylonians interchangeably. What little does survive pertaining to the identification of the Chaldeans suggests that they were an ethnic group separate and distinct from the Aramaeans. Whether Nabopolassar and Nebuchadnezzar were Chaldeans in the strict ethnic sense of the term or were "confused" with Chaldeans by the Greeks remains unclear. See J. A. Brinkman, *Prelude to Empire (=Occasional Publications of the Babylonian Fund* 7) (Philadelphia: 1984), 110-11.

4. Ibid., 37.

5. Ibid., 36-37.

6. See A. K. Grayson, *Assyrian and Babylonian Chronicles (=Texts from Cuneiform Sources,* vol. 5.) (Locust Valley: J. J. Augustin, 1975), 17 and 2, 87-88.

7. See Stanley M. Burstein, *The Babyloniaca of Berossus (=Sources From The Ancient Near East,* vol. 1, fasc. 5) (Malibu: Undena Publications, 1978), 26. For a brief discussion of the problem with the identification of Sarakos, Kandalanu, and others, see Brinkman, 110-11. See also Stefan Zawadzki, *The Fall of Assyria and Median-Babylonian Relations in Light of the Nabopolassar Chronicle* (Poznan: Adam Mickiewicz University Press, 1988), 144ff.

8. See Herodotus, *The Histories,* trans. A. D. Godley (London: William Heinemann, 1946), 1: 96ff.

9. The segment of Diodorus's *Universal History* translated here is from *Diodorus of Sicily,* trans. C. H. Oldfather (Cambridge, Mass.: Harvard University Press, 1933), 1: 429 and 431. Reprinted by permission of the publishers and the Loeb Classical Library.

10. Dandamaev, *Slavery,* 37ff.

11. See 2 Kings 23. 29; 2 Chron. 35. 20; Jer. 45.2; and Her. bk. 2.159. See also Donald J. Wiseman, *Chronicles of Chaldean Kings* (London: The British Museum, 1961), 24, 29ff, 84.

12. There is much contained in the writings of the Classical authors concerning Nebuchadnezzar's achievements. These sources are discussed at length in chap. 3.

13. Grayson, *Assyrian and Babylonian Chronicles*, 99-100.

14. See Alan Dundes, "What is Folklore?" in ed. Alan Dundes, *The Study of Folklore*, (Englewood Cliffs, N.J.: Prentice Hall, 1965), 1: "However, there has been no widespread agreement among folklorists about what folklore is. Not only do folklorists in different countries have different concepts of folklore, but also folklorists within one country may have quite diverse views concerning its nature."

15. See Barre Toelken, *The Dynamics of Folklore* (Boston, Houghton Mifflin, 1979), 28: "William Thoms, who made up the term *folklore* in the nineteenth century, and many of those who first became involved in the study of what were then called *popular antiquities*, were not trained as professionals in this field nor could they have anticipated the development of their elite hobby into a demanding academic discipline. As a result, subsequent folklorists have had to create their own conceptions of a field of inquiry along the way, often using terms (and biases) drawn from their own academic specialties."

16. See n. 18 below and also, in particular, Francis Lee Utley, "Folk Literature: An Operational Definition," in ed. Alan Dundes, *The Study of Folklore,* 7-24. See also William Bascom, "Folklore and Anthropology," in *Journal of American Folklore* 66 (1963): 283-90. Bascom's definition echoes Olrik's claim that stories originating with a written source are not necessarily folklore, even though folkloristic elements can clearly be distinguished in them. "Folklore, to the anthropologist, is a part of culture but not the whole of culture. It includes myths, legends, tales, proverbs, riddles, the texts of ballads and other songs, and other forms of lesser importance, but not folk art, folk dance, folk music, folk costume, folk medicine, folk custom, or folk belief . . . All folklore is orally transmitted but not all that is orally transmitted is folklore."

17. See Axel Olrik, "Epic Laws of Folk Narrative," in ed. Alan Dundes, *The Study of Folklore*, (Englewood Cliffs, N.J.: Prentice Hall, 1965), 131: "The common rules for the composition of all these *Sage* forms we can then call the *epic laws of folk narrative*. These laws apply to all European folklore and to some extent even beyond that." At the same time, Olrik points out (133) that the "entire world of folk narrative" does not conform to every "law," which raises a valid question as to the terminology used in his argument.

18. See A. Hultkrantz, *General Ethnological Concepts* (Copenhagen: Rosenkilde & Bagger, 1960), 126-41; E. Legros, *Sur les noms et les tendances du folklore* (Liege: ditions du Muse Wallon, 1962) and G. R. Simpson, *Herder's Concept of "Das Volk"* (Chicago: University of Chicago Libraries, 1921).

19. See Alan Dundes, "Who are the Folk?" in William R. Bascom, *The Frontiers of Folklore* (Boulder: Westview Press, 1977), 31ff.

20. See also Martin Schutze, "The Fundamental Ideas in Herder's Thought," in *Modern Philology* 19 (1921): 118, which points out that the early nineteenth century "regarded the folk and its creative, especially literary, products with contempt and derision, as lacking in refinement, learning, mastery of diction, and subtleness and elevation of thought. This aristocratic attitude toward folk literature is characteristic of the Rationalistic movement." Thus, Herder conceptualized folklore as being quite apart from a sophisticated literary tradition, and quite inferior to it at that. However,

as Dan Ben-Amos has pointed out, "The simplicity of folklore is in the eyes of the foreign beholder. Culturally, a folktale, a song, and a proverb can have as complex a system of meanings, connotations and significances, as any written work contemplated by a learned author . . . By the virtues of verbal creativity oral narratives have the same capabilities of multiplicity of meanings and intricacies of relations as any other form of verbal creation."

See Dan Ben-Amos, "The Context of Folklore: Implications and Prospects," in Bascom, *The Frontiers of Folklore*, 43.

21. See, in particular, Alan Dundes, "What is Folklore?" in ed. Alan Dundes, *The Study of Folklore*, 1ff.: "There are some forms of folklore which are manifested and communicated almost exclusively in written as opposed to oral form . . . In actual practice, a professional folklorist does not go so far as to say that a folktale or a ballad is not folklore simply because it has at some time in its life history been transmitted by writing or print."

22. See Toelken, *The Dynamics of Folklore*, 28-31. He also points out (32) that, "We might characterize or describe the materials of folklore as 'tradition-based communicative units informally exchanged in dynamic variation through space and time.' *Tradition* is here understood to mean not some static, immutable force from the past, but those pre-existing culture-specific materials and options that bear upon the performer more heavily than do his or her own personal tastes or talents. We recognize in the use of tradition that such matters as content and style have been for the most part passed on but not invented by the performer."

Chapter 2. The Cuneiform Sources

1. Samuel Noah Kramer, *The Sumerians* (Chicago: University of Chicago Press, 1963), 230.   For additional commentaries on the Sumerian Edubba, see Adam Falkenstein, "Der Sohn des Tafelhauses," in *Die Welt des Orients* 3 (1948): 172-86; Cyril J. Gadd, *Teachers and Students in the Oldest Schools* (London: School of Oriental and African Studies, University of London, 1956); Samuel Noah Kramer, *Schooldays* (Philadelphia: The University Museum, 1949).

2. See Gadd, *Teachers and Students*, 1ff. Although much has been written on the subject of teaching those who spoke Sumerian the art of writing the language, comparatively little has been done until recently to explain the method of scribal education after its demise as a spoken language.   See now the recent treatment of H. L. J. Vanstiphout, "How Did they Learn Sumerian?" *Journal of Cuneiform Studies* 31 (1979): 118ff.

3. Kramer, *The Sumerians*, 230ff. This did not preclude the broadening of the scribe's base to include the study and composition of literary works.

4. See Hermann Hunger, *Babylonische und Assyrische Kolophone, Alter Orient und Altes Testament* II (Neukirchen-Vluyn: Neukirchener Verlag, 1968); Adam Falkenstein, *Literarische Keilschrifttexte aus Uruk* (Berlin: 1931), 2ff.; F. Thureau-Dangin, *Tablettes d'Uruk   l'usage des prêtres du temple d'Anu au temps des Sélucides, Textes cunéiformes, Musée du Louvre*, 6 (Paris: 1922), 1ff.

5. For older analyses of the teaching of Sumerian, see F. R. Kraus, *Vom mesopotamischen Menschen der altbabylonischen Zeit und seiner Welt* (Amsterdam: 1973), 214-31; A. W. Sjöberg, "The Old Babylonian Edubba" in *Assyriological*

Studies 20 (Chicago: 1975), 159-79; S. N. Kramer, "The Sumerian School," in ed. G. E. Mylonas, *Studies Presented to David Moore Robinson*, (St. Louis: 1951), 243ff.; A. Falkenstein, "Die babylonische Schule," *Saeculum* 4 (1953): 125-37; and Gadd, *Teachers and Students.*

6. Vanstiphout, "How Did They Learn Sumerian?" 125.

7. A. Leo Oppenheim, *Ancient Mesopotamia: Portrait of a Dead Civilization* (Chicago: University of Chicago Press, 1964), 249.

8. Ibid, 242. See also Oppenheim's essay, "Man and Nature in Mesopotamian Civilization" in *Dictionary of Scientific Biography* 15, 364ff.

9. See David B. Weisberg, *Guild Structure and Political Allegiance in Early Achaemenid Mesopotamia, Yale Near Eastern Researches* I (New Haven: Yale University Press, 1967), 84. See also Samuel N. Kramer, *History Begins at Sumer* (New York: Doubleday, 1959), 1ff. See also the important treatment of H. M. Kümmel, *Familie, Beruf und Amt in Spätbabylonischen Uruk* (=*Abhandlungen der Deutschen Orient Gesellschaft*), Nr.20 (Berlin: Gebr. Mann Verlag, 1979).

10. Weisberg, *Guild Structure*, 81.

11. See R. P. Berger, *Die neubabylonischen Königsinschriften* (=*Alter Orient und Altes Testament*, vol. 4/1) (Neukirchen-Vluyn: Neukirchener Verlag, 1973), 75ff.

12. Ibid, 73, 81.

13. Ibid, 73-81.

14. Ibid, 81.

15. Axel Olrik, "Epic Laws of Folk Narrative," in ed. Alan Dundes, *The Study of Folklore,* (New Jersey: Prentice-Hall, 1965), 129.

16. See D. D. Luckenbill, *Annals of Sennacherib* (Chicago: University of Chicago Press, 1924) 3ff., and A. T. E. Olmstead, *Assyrian Historiography* (=*University of Missouri Studies*, 1916), 1-13, 22ff.

17. See Wiseman, *Chronicles of Chaldean Kings*, 1ff. and Grayson, *Assyrian and Babylonian Chronicles*, 8ff. See also Grayson, *Babylonian Historical Literary Texts* (Toronto: University of Toronto Press, 1975), 4ff. Reference will be made to this latter work in succeeding pages.

18. J. B. Pritchard, ed., *Ancient Near Eastern Texts Related to the Old Testament*, 2d ed. (Princeton: Princeton University Press, 1955), 307.

Text BM 33041 details an expedition of Nebuchadnezzar against Egypt in 568/7 B.C. "This is not part of the Babylonian Chronicle series but seems to be rather historical allusions in a religious text." For a translation, see Wiseman, 94ff., which includes a pertinent bibliography.

Note should be made here of the curious epic fragment regarding Amel-Marduk (which may have originally been about Nabonidus or Cyrus). This text probably belongs to the "apocalyptic" genre as well. See A. K. Grayson, *Babylonian Historical Literary Texts*, 21.

"The appearance of the Dynastic prophecy now adds significant evidence of this close connection. In the Dynastic prophecy the concept of the rise and fall of empires, which must have its roots in the dynastic tradition of Mesopotamian chronography, is mirrored by the similar concept in Daniel. Compare also the rubric regarding secrecy at the end of the Dynastic prophecy with the command in Daniel to keep the book sealed. But of prime significance is the possibility that the Dynastic prophecy concludes, as suggested both by internal evidence and on analogy with the prophecy in the Sibylline oracles, with a real attempt to predict the downfall of Hellenistic kings."

19. Ibid, 307.

20. Dandamaev, 7ff.   Mention should here also be made of the treatment of Jehoiachin, king of Judah, during his imprisonment in the reign of Nebuchadnezzar. See E. F. Weidner, "Jojachin, König von Juda, in babylonischen Keilinschrifttexten," *Mélanges syriens offerts à Monsieur René Dussaud*, 2 (Paris: 1939), 923-35.

21. Pritchard, *Ancient Near Eastern Texts*, 313.

22. The purpose (or purposes) of the journey of Nabonidus to Tema lies beyond the scope of this inquiry. For further information, see R. P. Dougherty, *Nabonidus and Belshazzar* (= *Yale Oriented Researches*, vol. 15) (New Haven: 1923), 153ff, and Julius Lewy, "The Assyro-Babylonian Cult of the Moon," in *Hebrew Union College Annual* 20 (1949), 435ff. See also S. A. Pallis, *The Babylonian Akitu Festival* (Copenhagen, 1926), 1ff.

23. Pritchard, *Ancient Near Eastern Texts*, 314.

24. In addition to the royal inscriptions, it should be noted that Nabonidus is prominent in many texts relating the contents of dreams. Reference will be made to the documents when discussing their relationship to the Hebrew sources. See below, Chap. 6, n. 27, which includes a bibliography.

25. Grayson, *Papyrus and Tablet*, 124.

26. Ibid, 126.   "The truth of the matter is that both texts, the Nabonidus Verse Account and the Cyrus Cylinder, were written to justify Cyrus's conquest of Babylonia.   The rationalization, or propaganda if one prefers, was done in a very clever way and it appears that Cyrus was wisely magnanimous in his treatment of the conquered state."

Note should be made here of another fragmentary text detailing the defeat of Nabonidus by Cyrus. It emphasizes the restoration of the ancient deities of Babylon by Cyrus and the return to the country of peace and stability. See Ibid, 123.

27. Ibid, 127.   "He (the god) showed Nabonidus, his reverent servant who looks after the shrines, the foundation of Naram-Sin, son of Sargon (of Akkad). In that year, in a favourable month, on a propitious day, without altering it one finger-length, Nabonidus laid its base on the foundation of Naram-Sin, son of Sargon—the foundation of Ebabbar, temple of Shamash. He discovered the inscription of Naram-Sin and, without altering it, restored it to its proper place." See Lambert, "A New Source for the Reign of Nabonidus," in *Archiv für Orientforschung*, 22 (1968/9): 1-8, 21-36.

As Grayson has noted (Ibid, 127-28), "Thus Nabonidus was not the consummate iconoclast portrayed by the Marduk priests. He had great respect for the religious customs and ancient history of Babylonia. It is apparent, therefore, that in their angry reaction to the denigration of Marduk, the Babylonian priests have absurdly overstated their case against Nabonidus."

See the text of Adad-guppi, mother of Nabonidus, in Ibid, 137. "The Word of Sin, king of the gods, which he spoke to me I heeded, and I myself saw it fulfilled. Nabonidus, my only son, the issue of my womb, perfected the neglected rites of Sin, Ningal, Nusku, and Sadarnunna. He rebuilt Ehulhul and finished that work. He entirely restored Harran so that it was better than before. He took the hand of Sin, Ningal, Nusku, and Sadarnunna from Babylon his royal city and settled them within Harran in Ehulhul, the dwelling which pleases them, with joy and rejoicing." See Pritchard, *Ancient Near Eastern Texts*, 3d ed., 560-62, and Gadd, "The Harran Inscriptions of Nabonidus," in *Anatolian Studies*, 8 (1958), 46-56.

For an attempt at the identification of Adad-guppi with the Nitocris of Herodotus, see W. Rllig, "Nitocris von Babylon" in *Beiträge zur Alten Geschichte und deren Nachleben* 1, (1969): 127-135. His arguments, however, are not exactly convincing.

28. The Book of Daniel pursues the negative tradition of Nabonidus under the name of Nebuchadnezzar. On the other hand, the "Prayer of Nabonidus" (found at Qumrân) portrays the king as a repentant and converted sinner. See Rudolf Meyer, *Das Gebet des Nabonid* (Berlin: 1962). This latter source carries forth the positive tradition that emphasizes his piety. Also see G. Vermes, *The Dead Sea Scrolls in English* (Baltimore: Penguin Books, 1962), 229; also below, chap. 6.

Chapter 3. Classical, Medieval, and Hebrew Sources

1. It is perhaps worth noting that, while both Herodotus and Xenophon deal with the neo-Babylonian period in their works, both focus their attention on the reign of Nabonidus (whom Herodotus calls Labynetus), the fall of Babylon, and the takeover of Cyrus. Neither author mentions by name or discusses the reign of Amel-Marduk. See George Rawlinson, *The History of Herodotus of Halicarnassus* (London: 1935), 1: 188-191 and Xenophon, *Cyropaedia*, trans. T. E. Page and W. H. D. Rouse (London: William Heinemann, 1912), 4:6 and 7:5.

Herodotus, as is the case with virtually all of the classical Greek authors, includes an elaborate description of Babylon, the temple of Bel (Belus), and the massive fortification walls surrounding the city. Such construction was of particular interest to the Greeks and it is not surprising, therefore, to find a folkloristic tradition developing around them. He seems to indicate that he visited the city. Strangely enough, neither Nebuchadnezzar nor Nabonidus is specifically related to this work; on the other hand, two queens, Semiramis and Nitocris, are said to have changed the course of the Euphrates and fortified Babylon with the intention of making it impregnable. See particularly Herodotus, *Histories*, 1:185. Mention of Semiramis can be found in Ctesias of Cnidus and in Diodorus Siculus, *Universal History*, 2. 4.20 as well as in Strabo, *Geography*, 4.

Semiramis (Assyrian Sammuramat, wife of Shamshi Adad V, 823-810 B.C.) was thought by the Greeks to be the daughter of a Syrian goddess Derceto, who was exposed at birth and tended by doves. For a bibliography of primary sources and commentaries on her era, see Borger, 3: 27ff. According to the Greeks, her first husband was Oannes and her second Ninus, thought to be king of Assyria and founder of Nineveh. Renowned as a builder of Babylon, she was changed into a dove at death. The "folklorizing" of Semiramis follows a distinct pattern adhered to strictly by classical Greek authors and reflects an infatuation with the conqueror or builder. See Lord Raglan, "The Hero of Tradition," in Dundes, 144ff. Berossus sought to separate fact from fancy by categorically denying the tales told of Semiramis (FHG 2: 507).

Several of the Jewish sources (no doubt as a result of Hellenistic influence and through preserving the accounts of Nebuchadnezzar found in Josephus's *Contra Apionem* and *Jewish Antiquities*) sought to equate Semiramis with Amytis, Nebuchadnezzar's Median wife, probably because of her desire to have the "Hanging Gardens" created to remind her of her homeland. See Strabo, *Geography*, 4.

2. Cary and Denniston, *The Oxford Classical Dictionary* (Oxford: The Clarendon Press, 1949), 553.

3. Flavius Josephus, *Contra Apionem*, in *The Works of Flavius Josephus*, English trans. H. St. John Thackeray (London: William Heinemann, 1926), 1: 20.

4. The English translation here is found in Isaac Cory, *Ancient Fragments of the Phoenician, Chaldean, Egyptian, Tyrian, Carthaginian, Indian, Persian and Other Writers* (London: 1876), 71-72. This fragment is preserved by Eusebius in Greek in his *Praeparatio Evangelica*, Caput 9:41 and in Latin (Jerome's translation) in the *Chronicorum*, Lib. 1, Caput 20: 3. See J. P. Migne, *Patrologia Cursus Completus, Series Graecae* (Paris: 1857), 19: 125-26.

5. Cory, *Ancient Fragments*, 71-72.

6. Mention of the relationship of "apocalyptic" or "prophetic" literature to the Achaemenid period in Uruk was first made by S. Kaufman and H. Hunger, "A New Akkadian Prophecy Text," *Journal of the American Oriental Society* (1975): 371ff., in which it was shown that this genre was represented in cuneiform documents as early as the sixth century, B.C. Since then, the penetrating analysis of A. K. Grayson (*Babylonian Historical Literary Texts*, 13ff.) has appeared and has shed new light on the whole question of the nature of information contained in several of the classical sources. For further discussion, see above, chap. 2.

7. Ibid, 24ff.

8. Ibid, 31-33.

9. Certainly, the tradition in the Book of Daniel associated the term *Chaldean* with a professional group rather than with an ethnic description (as Aramaeans).

10. See above, n. 1. For a discussion of Herodotus as a creature of his time, see A. de Sélincourt, *The World of Herodotus* (Boston: Little Brown & Co., 1962), 34-41, 53ff.

11. Josephus, *Contra Apionem*, 1: 19.

12. James Westfall Thompson, *A History of Historical Writing* (New York: Macmillan & Co., 1942), 12.

13. Cory, *Ancient Fragments*, 67. See Josephus, *Contra Apionem*, 1: 12-21 and Eusebius, *Chronicorum*, Lib. 1, Caput 11. Both the Greek text of Josephus and the Latin version of Eusebius can be found in Migne, 19: 126-31. See also Joanne Richter, *Berosi Chaldaeorum Historiae* (Lipsiae, 1825), 64-68, and Müller, *Fragmenta Historicorum Graecorum* (Paris: 1848), 2: 504-5.

14. This includes the reign of Nabopolassar, the founder of the dynasty. Berossus says he ruled twenty-one years, which is likewise corroborated by cuneiform sources. See Josephus, *Contra Apionem*, 1: 19, and Eusebius, *Chronicorum*, Lib. 1, Caput 11: 2. His commentary on Labashi-Marduk is also at least partially substantiated by cuneiform evidence. See Langdon, Nabonidus cylinder 5, col. 1.

15. See Parker and Dubberstein, *Babylonian Chronology 626 B.C. –A.D. 75. Brown University Studies* 19 (Providence: 1956), 13 who suggest that confusion may have been the result of the transmission of Berossus's manuscript (if, indeed, that manuscript originally contained numerals designating the reigns of each king.) A misreading of the numerals, then, might have occurred. However, their suggestion that a *theta* (ø) could have been mistaken for a *beta* (ß) does not necessarily follow, because two years are designated for Amel-Marduk, for which a *beta* would have been used.

16. See the discussion in Paul Schnabel, *Berossus und die babylonisch-hellenistische Literatur* (Hildesheim: Georg Olms, 1968), 273-75.

For an edition and study of Berossus, see Stanley M. Burstein, *The Babyloniaca of Berossus*, (*Sources From the Ancient Near East*, 1/5, 1978), 4ff. See also G. Komoroczy, "Berosos and the Mesopotamian Literature," in *Acta Antiqua* 21 (1973): 125ff. As Burstein notes (4), two groups of "Near Eastern intellectuals" attempted to relate to their Seleucid overlords. "One group created a literature, both oral and written, of protest, composing apocalyptic prophecies of the ultimate defeat of their oppressors on the one hand and elaborating still further the folk histories of the great heroes of their cultures' past on the other. Thus, new conquests were ascribed to Sesostris and Semiramis and alongside them chauvinistic new legends were formed around such figures as Rameses II and Nectanebo II in Egypt, Taharqa in Nubia, Moses and Abraham in Judea and Nebukadnezzar II in Babylon. The other group, however, more willing to cooperate with their new masters, attempted to educate them by the publication in Greek of authoritative accounts of their respective countries' history and culture, accounts in which the factual errors of the popular Greek authorities would be corrected; at the same time they provided an introduction to the authentic traditions of their civilizations. The compilation of such works was a genuine innovation, involving as it did the determination of what constituted the intellectual core of a civilization and the presentation of that core in a foreign language in such a way that it would be understood by readers almost totally ignorant of it."

For Berossus's education, see Komoroczy, 127-28. There are indications that Berossus composed his *Babyloniaca* in an attempt (in part at least) to induce Antiochus I to break with his predecessor's acts. See also A. Kuhrt, "Berossus' *Babyloniaka* and Seleucid Rule in Babylonia," in A. Kuhrt and S. Sherwin-White, *Hellenism in the East* (=*Hellenistic Culture and Society*, 2). (Berkeley: University of California Press, 1987), 53-56.

17. Cary and Denniston, *Oxford Classical Dictionary*, 35. For a commentary on Alexander Polyhistor and his value as a historian, see Felix Jacoby, *Fragmenta der griechischen Historiker* (Leiden: E. J. Brill, 1964), Dritter Teil A., 259ff.

18. Thompson, *History of Historical Writing*, 13.

19. The English translation of the Armenian version of Eusebius's *Chronicle* is from Cory, *Ancient Fragments*, 87-88. Cory used Auchers's edition of the *Chronicle* published in Venice in 1818, 44-45. A more readily available translation of the Armenian version of the *Chronicle* (in German) has been done by J. Karst, *Eusebius' Werke V, Die Chronik aus dem Armenischen übersetzt* (Leipzig, 1911). For the Latin version of Polyhistor, see Migne, 19: 119 (Eusebius's *Chronicorum*, Lib. 1, Caput 6, 5). See also Eusebius Pamphili, *Eusebii Chronicorum Libri Duo*, ed., A. Schöne, 2 vols. (Berlin, 1866), and particularly S. Hieronymus, "Hieronymi Chronicon," 2 ed., in R. Helm, ed., *Die griechischen christlichen Schriftsteller der ersten Jahruhunderte, Eusebius' Werke*, vol. 7 (Berlin, 1956).

20. A. T. E. Olmstead, *Assyrian Historiography* (*University of Missouri Studies*, 1916), 63.

21. For an exhaustive treatment of Eupolemus and his possible sources, see Ben Zion Wacholder, *Eupolemus A Study of Judaeo-Greek Literature* (Cincinnati: Hebrew Union College Press, 1974), 25ff.

22. Ibid, 245.

23. Ibid, 231ff. where the problems concerning the identification of the Greek sources used by Eupolemus are discussed. See especially, 232-33: "We have other indications that Eupolemus had before him a book that had fused the accounts of Herodotus and Ctesias with some native Babylonian and Jewish traditions. . . .Such reliable information could have become available to Eupolemus only from a native

source, which may have already fused Herodotus and Ctesias with accounts based on old Babylonian records."

24. See, for example, Ibid, 230: "But when Nebuchadnezzar. . . , the king of the Babylonians, heard of Jeremiah's prediction, he summoned Astibares, king of the Medes, to join him in a campaign."

25. See Ibid, 230: "It appears, moreover, that Eupolemus was contrasting the contemporary impotence of the Jewish state with its supposedly former status of great power. In preparation for war with Jonachim, Nebuchadnezzar made certain that his Median allies would join him in the campaign: 'After having collected both Medians and Babylonians, he (Nebuchadnezzar) collected 180,000 foot soldiers, 120,000 horsemen, and 10,000 chariots for the infantry.' There is nothing in our biblical sources to suggest that the Medians participated in the destruction of Jerusalem. Neither does Scripture record the tribal or numerical composition of the Babylonian forces."

26. For further examples and discussion of similar cuneiform apocalyptic texts, see H. Hunger and S. Kaufman, "A New Akkadian Prophecy Text," *Journal of the American Oriental Society* 95 (1975): 372ff.; W. G. Lambert, *The Background of Jewish Apocalyptic* (London: Athlone Press, 1978), 11ff., and R. H. Sack, "The Temple Scribe in Chaldean Uruk," in *Visible Language* 15, no. 4 (1981): 409ff.

27. Thompson, *History of Historical Writing*, 105.

28. See n. 24.

29. Flavius Josephus, *Jewish Antiquities*, in *The Works of Flavius Josephus*, trans. Ralph Marcus (Cambridge, Mass.: Harvard University Press, 1937), 6: 285 and 287. Reprinted by permission of the publishers and the Loeb Classical Library.

30. See Bedae, "Chronicorum," in *Chronica Minora*, vol. 3 in Theodor Mommsen, *Monumenta Germaniae Historica* (Berlin: Apud. Weidmannof, 1898), 9: 269, 146, 270, 149. The exact same words occur here.

31. μῆτε προστιθεὶς τοῖς πραγμάσιν αὐτὸς ἰδία (*Jewish Antiquities*, 1: 17).

32. William Smith and Henry Wace, *Dictionary of Christian Biography* (London: John Murray, 1882), 452.

33. Louis Feldman, "Scholarship on Philo and Josephus 1937-1959" in *The Classical World*, vol. 55, no. 8-9, May 1962 and June 1962, 236ff, 278ff. Unfortunately, this is only a bibliographical essay rather than an attempt to deal with the problem itself. See now the treatment of Harold W. Attridge, *The Interpretation of Biblical History in the Antiquitates Judaicae of Flavius Josephus* (=*Harvard Dissertations in Religion*, 7). (Missoula, Scholar's Press, 1976.)

34. I. Epstein, ed., *The Babylonian Talmud* (London: Soncino Press, 1938), *Megillah* 11b.

35. Rabbi Dr. H. Freedman, *Midrash Rabbah* (London: Soncino Press, 1901). See in particular 2 *Targum Esther* 1.1 (9: 44), *Bereshit Rabbah* 44. 15 (1: 370), and esp. *Esther Rabbah* 3. 1 8 (9: 51), and *Esther Rabbah, Proem*, 12 (9: 17) in which it is implied that Belshazzar was the son of Amel-Marduk.

36. See Alfred Rahlfs, *Septuaginta* (Stuttgart, Priviligierte Wurttembergische Bibelanstalt) *Baruch* 1. 1-15. This account is probably based on Dan. 5-6, in which only Nebuchadnezzar and Belshazzar are mentioned.

37. Thackeray seems to be in accord with this judgment, but goes a step further: "Anyhow, he has to attract his Greek readers, diversified the record with a mass of legendary matter, which is of considerable interest to us. He has called from all quarters. . .But a large proportion find parallels, or partial parallels, in the Rabbinic

works, which were not compiled until a century or more later, and these, with other traditions for which no parallel can be traced, may be regarded as a valuable collection of first century Midrash." See H. St. John Thackeray, *Josephus, the Man and the Historian* (New York: Jewish Institute of Religion Press, 1929), 91.

The subject of Jehoiachin's release from prison and the relationship of Josephus's account of it to the Bible and rabbinical sources will be treated more fully later.

Josephus's identification of Nabonidus and Belshazzar may again reflect the Jewish knowledge of both the positive and negative traditions regarding Nabonidus. In Josephus, Belshazzar appears as the arch-desecrator. It is possible that Josephus uses the tradition regarding Nabonidus' irregular religious activities as a neat fix on Belshazzar as a historical character, thus leaving Nebuchadnezzar "clean." If this interpretation is correct, then the Old Testament writer attached the Nabonidus legends to Nebuchadnezzar, while Josephus associated them with Belshazzar—again, for different reasons.

For a discussion of the *Prayer of Nabonidus* and the possible relationship of its contents to Daniel 2-6, see above, 69.

38. See κλαυδίοου πτολεμαίου μαθηματικὴ σύνταξις, *Composition Mathematique de Claude Ptolemée*, ed., M. Halma (Paris: Chez Henry Grande, Librairie, 1813), 1: 71. See also E. J. Bickerman, *Chronology of the Ancient World* (Ithaca: Cornell University Press, 1968), 108. His precision suggests that he either had access to the documents themselves or perhaps utilized an intermediary source (now lost) based on the dates given in the documents.

For a recent discussion of the *Ptolemaic Conon*, see A. K. Grayson, "Königlisten und Chroniken," in *Reallexikon der Assyriologie*, 5 (1980).

39. See n. 33.

40. "Abydenos," in George Wissowa, *Realencyclopaedie der classischen Altertumswissenchaft* (Stuttgart: J. B. Metzherscher Verlag, 1894), 1: 130. See also n. 24. Beyond this, nothing relevant to this period from *About the Assyrians* has survived.

41. Philip Schaff and Henry Wace, *A Select Library of the Nicene and Post Nicene Fathers of the Christian Church* (Grand Rapids: William Beerdman's Publishing Co., 1961), 1: 31.

42. See Thompson, *History of Historical Writing*, 129.

For a superb treatment of Eusebius's *Chronicle* and the question of sources used in its writing, see Alden A. Mosshammer, *The Chronicle of Eusebius and Greek Chronographic Tradition* (Lewisburg: Bucknell University Press, 1979). Included here is a discussion of the relationship of the works of Thallus, Castor, Prophyry, and Julius Africanus to the information regarding the ancient Near East included in Eusebius's *Chronicle*. An excellent summary of the manuscript tradition and the contents of previously published editions is included, as well as an up-to-date bibliography.

43. See ns. 20, 23, 24, and 29. Eusebius also mentions (though only briefly) Amel-Marduk in bk. 2 of his *Chronicle*. See Migne, vol. 19. 465-66. Another edition of Eusebius's *Chronicle*, bk. 2, was published by John Knight Fotheringham, *Eusebii Pamphili Chronici* (London: Humphrey Milfor, 1923), 178, 22. Here the following interesting words appear: "Mortuo Nabuchodonosor Babyloniorum rege suscepti imperium Evilmerodach. Cui successit frater eius Baltasar." This statement of Eusebius (that Amel-Marduk was the brother of Belshazzar) does not agree with either

the Book of Daniel, the apocryphal *Book of Baruch*, or the midrash *Esther Rabbah* (a source composed much later) in which it is implied that Belshazzar was Amel-Marduk's son. See n. 30.

44. See S. Hieronymi, *Presbyteri Opera Commentarium in Danielem II*, Visio 5.1, in *Corpus Christianorum Series Latina* (Turnholti: Typographi Brepobs Editores Pontifici, 1964), 75A: 820. Here the following words appear: post Nabuchodonosor, qui regnavit annis quadraginta tribus, successisse in regnum eius filium qui vocabatur Evchil-marodach—de quo scribit et Ieremias: quod in primo anno regni sui levaverit caput regis Iudae et eduxerit eum de domo carceris in regno patris successerit filius eius Neglisar, post rursum filius eius Labor-sordech, quo mortuo, Baltasar filius eius regnum tenuerit quem nunc scriptura commemorat.

45. S. Hieronymi, *Presbyteri Opera Commentarium in Esaiam V*, Vision 14.19, in Ibid, 75: 169-170. See also Louis Ginsberg, *The Legends of the Jews* (Philadelphia: The Jewish Publication Society of America, 1946), 6: 427-28.

46. For a discussion of the composition of the *Liber Genealogus*, see Theodor Mommsen, "Auctores Antiquissimi," in *Monumenta Germaniae Historica* (Berlin: Apud. Weidmanoff, 1892), 9: 78.

47. "Liber Genealogus," in Georg Wissowa, *Realencyclopaedie der classischen Altertumswissenschaft* (Stuttgart: J. B. Metzherscher Verlag, 1913), 8: 1878. For a discussion of the relationship of the *Liber Genealogus* to the *Chronicle of Fredegar*, see J. M. Wallace-Hadrill, *The Fourth Book of the Chronicle of Fredegar* (London: Thomas Nelson & Sons, Ltd., 1960), 11, in which the sources of the *Chronicle* are discussed. See also the prologue to the *Chronicle* itself (p. 1) in which the author(s) states, "I have most carefully read the chronicle of St. Jerome, of Hydatius, of a certain wise man, of Isidore and Gregory, from the beginning of the world to the decline of Guntramm's reign." The "certain wise man," says Walter Goffart in "The Fredegar Problem Reconsidered" in *Speculum* (April, 1963): 210, "is almost certainly the anonymous author of *Liber Generationis*." Further comments may be found in Wattenbach and Levison, *Deutschlands Geschichtsquellen im Mittelalter bis zur Mitte des dreizehnten Jahrhunderts* (Weimar: Herman Bohlaus Nachfolger, 1952), 1: 54, and an excellent review of the possible sources used by the composer of the *Liber Generationis* can be found in Martin Schanz, *Geschichte der römischen Literatur* (Munich: 1914) 4 Teil, I. Band, 64-65, 516-17.

48. See "Liber Generationis" in *Chronica Minora*, vol. 1 in Theodor Mommsen, *Monumenta Germaniae Historica* (Berlin: Apud. Weidmannof, 1892), 9: 181. It should be noted, however, that an interval of thirty years is mentioned separating the beginning of the Captivity and the release of Jehoiachin, whereas in the Bible it is thirty-seven years.

49. See n. 39.

50. For the precise location of these references in Bede's *Chronicle*, see 55. For an English translation, see J. A. Giles, *The Historical Works of Venerable Bede* (London: James Bohn, 1845), 242-43.

51. M. L. W. Laistner, "Bede as a Classical and Patristic Scholar" in *Transactions of the Royal Historical Society*, 4th Ser., 16: 78. For a commentary on the problems of Bede's sources in general, consult Charles W. Jones, "Bedae Opera de Temporibus," in *Medieval Academy of America*, vol. 41 (Cambridge: 1943), 38-41.

52. "Chronicon Paschale," in Georg Wissowa, *Realencyclopaedie der classischen Altertumswissenschaft* (Stuttgart: J. B. Metzhersher Verlag, 1899), 2: 2459ff.

53. See "Chronicon Alexandrinum" in *Chronica Minora*, vol. 1, in Theodor Mommsen, *Monumenta Germaniae Historica*, 9: 128. It was first published under the title by the Jesuit Rader in 1615. It appears in the above work as the *Barbarus Scaliergi*.

54. Carl Krumacher, "Geschichte der byzantinischen Literatur," in I. von Müller, *Handbuch der classichen Altertumswissenschaft* (Munich: C.H. Becksche Verlagsbuchhandlung, 1897), Bd. 9, Abt. 1, 337.

55. See Heinrich Gelzer, *S. Julius Africanus und die byzantinische Chronographie* (Leipzig: 1880), Bd. 1, 180ff.

56. See 55 and n. 114.

57. "Chronicon Paschale" in B. G. Neibuhr, ed., *Corpus Scriptorum Historiae Byzantinae* (Bonnae: Impensis Ed., Weberi, 1831), 16: 257, 15 (138a).

58. See n. 43 and Ibid, 258.

59. Georgius Syncellus, "Chronographia" in B. G. Niebuhr, *Corpus Scriptorum Historiae Byzantinae* (Bonnae: Impensis Ed. Weberi, 1829), 12: 390-91.

60. See Bickerman, *Chronology*, 108 to compare the figures Syncellus cites with those in the *Ptolemaic Canon* as it has come down to us through other channels.

61. Syncellus, "Chronographia" in Niebuhr, *Corpus Scriptorum Historiae Byzantinae*, 393.

62. Ibid, 421-22.

63. Ibid, 427.

64. See Ibid, 426-28.

65. See Ibid, 426-27.

66. See particularly Ibid, 427-28, in which he distorts Berossus and Josephus while adding the equation Nabonidus = Astyages = Xerxes = Darius.

67. J.W. Bosanquet, "Cyrus the Second" *Transactions of the Society of Biblical Archaeology*, 1(1872): 247.

68. See Ibid, 262 and Dougherty, *Nabonidus and Belshazzar*, 13-14.

69. See 62ff.

70. See discussions of the Talmud and the *Chronicle of Jerachmeel*, as well as ns. 86, 112-13.

71. "Talmud," in Isidore Singer, et al., *The Jewish Encyclopaedia* (New York: Funk & Wagnalls, 1909), 12: 1.

72. "Megillah" in Ibid, 8: 425-26.

73. Epstein, *Babylonian Talmud*, 65-66.

74. "Midrash" in Singer, et al., *The Jewish Encyclopaedia*, 8:549.

75. Ibid, 552.

76. Ibid, 549.

77. Freedman, *Bereshit Rabbah*, 1:28.

78. "Midrash" in Singer et al., 8: 561.

79. Freedman, *Bemidbar Rabbah*, 5: 7.

80. Ibid, 8: 7 and 9: 7.

81. See John Bowker, *The Targums and Rabbinic Literature* (Cambridge: University Press, 1969), 79.

82. Ibid, 82.

83. Ibid, 84.

84. Ibid, 83.

85. Here it will be remembered that Amel-Marduk was said to have ruled in an unjust manner (Josephus, *Contra Apionem* 1: 20), but the *Bereshit Rabbah* contrasts

Amel-Marduk with Nebuchadnezzar and Belshazzar, who are referred to as "two wicked men, two destroyers." See *Bereshit Rabbah*, 85.2 in Freedman, 2: 789.

86. Ibid, 1: 370.

87. See Wayikra Rabbah 18.2 in Ibid, 4: 229 in which the following words appear: "When Nebuchadnezzar died they again approached Evil Merodach to appoint him king. Said he to them, 'I shall not heed you; the first time, after I hearkened to you, he took me and imprisoned me, this time he will slay me.' And he did not believe them until they dragged Nebuchadnezzar forth and cast him before him."

88. See 2 *Targum Esther* 1.1 and *Esther Rabbah* 2, 1.8 in Ibid, 9: 33, 44. Here the mention of Amel-Marduk as "cosmocrator" also occurs.

89. "Midrash" in Singer, et al., 553. See also Bowker, *The Targums*, 74-76.

90. August Wünsche, *Pesiqta des Rab Kahana* (Leipzig: Otto Schulze, 1885), 2: 14a. Compare the following words to those contained in 2 *Targum Esther* 1.1: "Da sprach Gott zu ihm: 'Weil du von deinem Throne dich erhoben und meinetwegen drei Schritte gethan hast, so werde ich, bei meinem Leben schwöre ich es! Drei Könige vor dir erstehen lassen, welche gewaltige Herrscher (Kosmokratoren) von einem Ende der Welt bis zum anderen sein werden. Dieselben sind Nebuchadnezzar, Evil Merodach und Belshazzar.'"

For editions of the *Pesiqta*, see Bernard Mandelbaum, ed., *Pesikta de-Rab Kahana* (New York, 1962), 2 vols.; W. G. Braude, *Pesikta Rabbati* (New Haven, Yale University Press, 1968), 2 vols.; and for dates of composition, see E. Schrer, *The History of the Jewish People in the Age of Jesus Christ* rev. and ed. G. Vermes and F. Millar (Edinburgh: T & T Clark, 1973).

91. "Tanhuma," in Singer, et al., 12: 44-45. See also "Tanhuma" in Isaac Landman, *The Universal Jewish Encyclopaedia* (New York: Universal Jewish Encyclopaedia, 1943), 10: 169.

92. "Tanhuma" in Singer, et al., 12: 44-45.

93. Ibid, 45. For precise references in Tanhuma to Amel-Marduk and Jehoiachin, consult Ginsberg, *Legends of the Jews*, 6: 427.

94. Meyer Waxman, *A History of Jewish Literature* (New York, Bloch Publishing Co., 1930), 1: 421.

95. "Seder ᶜOlam Zuta," in Singer, et al., 12: 149.

96. See Ginsberg, *Legends of the Jews*, 6: 428.

97. See Ibid, Jer. 52:31 states that Jehoiachin was released on the twenty-fifth day of the twelfth month in the thirty-seventh year of the Captivity, while 2 Kings 25:27 says he was released two days later.

98. "Seder ᶜOlam Zuta," in G. Genebrardi, *Chronologia Hebraeorum* (Paris, 1572), 110.

99. "Abot de-Rabbi Nathan" in Singer, et al., 1: 82.

100. See Ginsberg, *Legends of the Jews*, 6: 380, 428, in which pertinent quotations from the second recension of *Abot de-Rabbi Nathan* are given. According to 2 *ARN* 17 37, Amel-Marduk wanted to set Jehoiachin at liberty because he had been imprisoned by Nebuchadnezzar without cause. The high officials of the state were upset, however, and asserted that "A king cannot revoke the edicts of his predecessor, unless he drags the corpse of the dead king out of the grave." This he proceeded to do.

101. "Jerachmeel ben Solomon," in Jakob Klatzkin, *Encyclopaedia Judaica* (Berlin: Verlag Esckol, 1931), 8: 1083.

102. Moses Gaster, *The Chronicle of Jerachmeel* (London: Royal Asiatic Society, 1899), 207.

103. Ibid, 206-7. It also should be noted that Jerachmeel's tale about Amel-Marduk regarding his removal of Nebuchadnezzar's corpse from the grave (mentioned in this section of the *Chronicle*) probably came from either the *Wayikra Rabbah* or 2 *Abot de-Rabbi Nathan*. He adds, however, that it was Jehoiachin who told Amel-Marduk to remove the corpse. This is not found in any other source.

104. For a summary of theories developed by historians over the past century concerning the neo-Babylonian and Persian periods, see Dougherty, *Nabonidas and Belshazzar*, 13-14 and particularly H. H. Rowley, *Darius the Mede* (New York, 1964).

105. See Louis F. Hartman, *The Book of Daniel* (=*Anchor Bible*, vol. 23) (Garden City: Doubleday and Co., 1978), 174ff. See also J. T. Milik, "Priére de Nabonide," in *Revue Biblique*, (1956), 407ff. and Pierre Grelot, "La Priére de Nabonide" (4 Q or Nab) *Revue de Qumrân* 9, no. 4 (1978): 483-95.
This *Prayer of Nabonidus* may also explain why the characterization of Nebuchadnezzar is somewhat muted in the Book of Daniel in contrast to that of the figure of Belshazzar. Again, this may point to the identification by the Old Testament writer of the "real" Nebuchadnezzar with Nabonidus.

106. See R.H. Charles, *The Apocrypha and Pseudoepigraphia of the Old Testament* (Oxford: The Clarendon Press, 1976), 1: 569-82, 538ff., 2: 470-80, 522, 527-33. See also M. J. H. Charlesworth, *The Pseudoepigraphia and Modern Research* (Chico: Scholars Press, 1981).

107. Ibid, 1: 174-201, 239ff.

108. Ibid, 1: 1-19, 26.

109. Ibid, 1: 596ff., 599.

110. Ibid, 1: 242ff.,249-54.

111. Ibid, 2: 715-22, 754. See also James Lindenberger, *The Aramaic Proverbs of Ahiqar* (Baltimore: The Johns Hopkins University Press, 1983).

112. See Charles C. Torrey, *The Lives of the Prophets* (=*Journal of Biblical Literature Monograph Series*, vol. 1) (Philadelphia, 1946), 3-17.

113. Ibid, 39. This work is not a series of biographies, but a repository of Jewish traditions not embodied in the canonical Book of Daniel. ("The Names of the Prophets, whence they were, where they died, and how and where they were buried".) The author is, of course, familiar with the Old Testament. He writes the following about Nebuchadnezzar and Daniel.

He made great supplication in behalf of Nebuchadnezzar, whose son Belshazzar besought him for aid at the time when the king became a beast of the field, lest he should perish. For his head and foreparts were those of an ox, his legs and hinder parts those of a lion. The meaning of this marvel was revealed to the prophet: the king became a beast, because of his self-indulgence and his stubbornness. It is the manner of tyrants, that in their youth they come under the yoke of Satan; in their latter years they become wild beasts, snatching, destroying, smiting, and slaying.

The prophet knew by divine revelation that the king was eating grass like an ox, and that it became for him the food of a human being. Therefore it was that Nebuchadnezzar himself, recovering human reason when digestion was completed, used to weep and beseech the Lord, praying forty times each day and night. Then the mind of a dumb animal would (again) take possession of him and he would forget that he had been a human being. His tongue had lost the power of speech; when he understood his condition he wept, and his eyes were like raw flesh from his weeping.

Daniel caused seven years (the meaning of his "seven times") to become seven months. The mystery of the seven times was fulfilled upon the king, for in seven months he was restored and in the (remaining) six years and five months he was doing penance to the Lord and confessing his wickedness. When his sin had been forgiven, the Kingdom was given back to him. He ate neither bread nor flesh in the time of his repentance, for Daniel had bidden him eat pulse and greens while appeasing the Lord.

For an Arabic recension, see O. Lofgren, *An Arabic Recension of the Vitae Prophetarium,* in *Orientalia Suecana* 25-27: 77-105.

114. The name of Nebuchadnezzar occurs in the following books of the Old Testament:

1. 2 Kings 24 and 25 and 2 Chronicles 36:6ff. The two campaigns of Nebuchadnezzar against Jerusalem are included.
2. Ezra 1, 2, and 5. The return of the Jews to Palestine is detailed.
3. Nehemiah 7:6ff. Included here is a register of those who returned from Jerusalem.
4. Esther 2:6. Nebuchadnezzar is mentioned here only in passing.
5. Jeremiah 27-52. This contains the prophecy of the destruction of Jerusalem.
6. Ezekiel 30:10. The destruction of Egypt is foretold by Nebuchadnezzar.
7. Daniel 1-6. This book has the most complete characterization of Nebuchadnezzar found in the Hebrew sources.

115. Ibid, 98. "In some book I have found tables illustrative of the durations of the reigns of the kings of the Assyrians, i.e., the people of Mosul, of the kings of the Copts, who reigned in Egypt, and the Ptolemaean princes, each of whom was called Ptolemaeus. . . .In the same book I have found the chronology of the later kings of the Greeks.

"Now I have transferred those identical tables into this place of my book. . .For they are corrupted by the tradition of the copyists, when they pass from hand to hand among them. Their emendation is a work of many years."

Following this is a collection of king lists, including that beginning with Nabonasir. See 100ff.

116. Ibid, 297.

117. See P. Hitti, *History of the Arabs* (London: MacMillan & Co., 1961), 390-91. See also M. J. De Goeje, et al., *Annales* (Leiden: Brill, 1881), prima series, 2: 645.

118. See Hitti, *History of the Arabs,* 391.

119. See B. Lewis, et al., *The Encyclopaedia of Islam* (Leiden: Brill, 1971), 2: 844-5.

Certainly the written prototype for the Ahiqar legend was in Aramaic originally. However, these documents were composed on perishable material and are now lost.

This is true of the Semiramis story as well. See Komoroczy, "Ein assyrischer König in der arabischen überlieferung" in *Altorientalische Forschungen* 1 (1974): 153-64.

Chapter 4. Nebuchadnezzar the Destroyer

1. See the thorough and detailed analysis of the events (recorded in the cuneiform chronicles) of Nebuchadnezzar's early years in Donald J. Wiseman, *Chronicles of Chaldean Kings* (London: The British Museum, 1961), 27ff. As the purpose of this volume and chapter is somewhat different than that of a straight historical narrative, the reader is referred to Wiseman's excellent commentary for knowledge of each event.

2. Ibid, 27.

3. Grayson, *Assyrian and Babylonian Chronicles*, chron. 5, 99 (=BM 21946, obverse, 1.1-8). See also 98 (=chron. 4, BM 22047), l. 24-28: "The army of Egypt, which was in Carchemish, crossed the Euphrates and marched against the army of Akkad which was camped in Quramatu. They pushed the army of Akkad back so that they withdrew. The twenty-first year: The king of Akkad stayed home (while) Nebuchadnezzar (II), his eldest son (and) crown prince, mustered the army of Akkad."

4. Wiseman, *Chronicles*, 28.

5. Ibid, 28.

6. Grayson, *Assyrian and Babylonian Chronicles*, chron. 5, 100.

7. Ibid, 101. See also Wiseman, *Chronicles*, 26, in which it is suggested that Nebuchadnezzar did not enter Judah at this time but that the taking of Syria compelled Jehoiakim of Judah to become subject to Nebuchadnezzar's authority. See 2 Kings 24:7 – "And the king of Egypt did not come again out of his land, for the king of Babylon had taken all that belonged to the king of Egypt from the Brook of Egypt to the river Euphrates." Whether the reference (in 1 Dan. 1) to the taking of some Jewish captives to Babylonia refers to this time (605 B.C.) as Wiseman suggests is questionable.

8. Grayson, *Assyrian and Babylonian Chronicles*, chron. 5, 101.

9. Ibid, 101. Sennacherib, among others, also plundered kingdoms in the area of Arabia. See, for example, the account of his first campaign in D. D. Luckenbill, *The Annals of Sennacherib* (Chicago: University of Chicago Press, 1924), 54: "The Arabs, Aramaeans, Chaldeans, who were in Uruk, Nippur, Kish, Harsagkalamma, together with the citizens, the rebels (sinners), I brought forth and counted as spoil."

10. Grayson, *Assyrian and Babylonian Chronicles*, chron. 5 101.

11. See below, chap. 6.

12. See Stanley M. Burstein, *The Babyloniaca of Berossus* (=*Sources from the Ancient Near East*, vol. 1, fasc. 5) (Malibu: Undena Publications, 1978), 26.

13. Ibid, 27, and n. 104, in which Burstein points out the difficulty with this passage. "As Josephus (*Against Apion* 1.145) cited this passage in support of the biblical account of the sack of Jerusalem in 586, it is clear that Polyhistor's epitome of Berossus contained no further information on Nebukadnezzar's western campaigns." Because Tatian derived *his* information from another source, Juba's *Concerning the Assyrians*, it should be obvious that this whole account is difficult to interpret. Perhaps one could be so bold as to suggest that here we have a *conflation* of the initial campaign against Necho II *before* Nebuchadnezzar ascended the throne of Babylon and

an account of a second campaign (presumably in 586 B.C.), the result of which was a deportation of captives to Babylon.

14. Megasthenes, *History of India*, preserved by Eusebius, *Praeparatio Evangelica*, bk. 10 and quoted in Cory, *Ancient Fragments*, 71.

15. S. K. Eddy, *The King is Dead: Studies in the Near Eastern Resistance to Hellenism 334-31 B.C.* (Lincoln: University of Nebraska Press, 1961), 125-26. See also Burstein, *Babyloniaca*, 25, who points out that "In Berossus's day *Coele Syria* was a geographical term referring to that portion of southern Syria and Palestine occupied by Ptolemy I in 301 but claimed by the Seleucids, roughly the territory between Sidon and Egypt." See also F. W. Walbank, *A Historical Commentary on Polybius* (Oxford, 1957), 1: 564, and Benjamin Mazar, "The Aramaean Empire and its Relations with Israel," in *Biblical Archaeologist*, 25 (1962): 119-20.

16. See the treatment of Harold W. Attridge, *The Interpretation of Biblical History in the Antiquitates Judaicae of Flavius Josephus* (=*Harvard Dissertations in Religion*, no. 7) (Missoula: Scholars Press, 1976), 34ff.

17. Flavius Josephus, *Jewish Antiquities*, trans. Ralph Marcus (Cambridge, Mass.: Harvard University Press, 1937), 6: 205.

18. See above, chap. 3, 48.

19. Flavius Josephus, *Jewish Antiquities*, 6: 207. "And this was what the prophet Jeremiah foretold day after day how that it was vain for them to cling to their hope of help from Egyptians and that the city was destined to be overthrown by the king of Babylonia and King Joakeimos to be subdued by him."

20. Ibid, 6: 207 and 209.

21. See Thackery's comments on this subject quoted above, chap. 3, 85.

22. Grayson, *Assyrian and Babylonian Chronicles*, chron. 5, 102.

23. Wiseman, *Chronicles*, 35, although this does not agree with the account given in Josephus, *Jewish Antiquities*, 6:211 and 213. Three thousand captives, says Josephus, were deported to Babylon, among them the prophet Ezekiel.

24. 2 Kings 24:17 and Jeremiah 37:1. In 2 Kings 24:14-16, it is stated that Nebuchadnezzar took over 18,000 captives, including Jehoiachin and his family. Jehoiachin remained imprisoned in Babylon until he was released by Amel-Marduk, Nebuchadnezzar's son, thirty-seven years later.

25. Josephus, *Jewish Antiquities*, 6: 211, 213, and 215.

26. The prophecy of Jeremiah, recorded by Polyhistor, is preserved by Eusebius, and begins with the same language used by Eupolemus—"Jonachin then attempted to burn him alive: but he said that with that fuel they should cook food for the Babylonians, and as prisoners of war should dig the canals of the Tigris and Euphrates. When Nebuchadnezzar, king of the Babylonians, had heard of the predictions of Jeremiah, he summoned Astibares, the king of the Medes, to join him in an expedition."

See Eusebius, *Preparation for the Gospel*, trans. Edwin Hamilton Gifford (Grand Rapids: Baker Book House, 1981), pt. 1. 486 (bk. 9, chap. 39, 454b).

27. See Eupolemus, *Concerning the Kings in Judea*, in *Fragments from Hellenistic Jewish Authors*, vol. 1: *Historians*, Carl R. Holladay (Chico, CA: Scholars Press, 1984), frag. 4, 133-35.

28. See the penetrating analysis of Hellenic and Mesopotamian historiography in John VanSeters, *In Search of History* (New Haven: Yale University Press, 1983), 8-99.

29. Ezekiel 12. 13: "And I will bring him to Babylon, to the land of the Chaldeans yet shall he not see it though he shall die there."

30. Jeremiah 34. 3: "And thou shalt not escape out of his hand but shalt surely be taken and delivered into his hand; and thine eyes shall behold the king of Babylon and thy mouth shall speak to his mouth and thou shalt come to Babylon."

31. Josephus, *Jewish Antiquities*, 6: 217: "After maintaining his alliance with the Babylonians for eight years, Sacchias broke his treaty with them and went over to the Egyptians, hoping to overthrow the Babylonians if he joined the other side."

32. Ibid, 6: 217 and 219. "But, when the Egyptian king heard of the plight of his ally Sacchias, he raised a large force and came to Judaea to end the siege. Thereupon the Babylonian king left Jerusalem and went to meet the Egyptians and, encouraging them in battle, defeated and put them to flight and drove them out of the whole of Syria."

33. Ibid, 6: 229 and 231.

34. It appears that this information is erroneously related to the time of Nabopolassar and is the result of Josephus's own interpolation of Jewish oral and written tradition. See Josephus, *Against Apion*, trans. H. St. John Thackeray (London: William Heinemann, 1926), bk. 1. 130-31.

35. See 1 Esdras 1.34-58 in R. H. Charles, *The Apocrypha and Pseudoepigraphia of the Old Testament* (Oxford: The Clarendon Press, 1976), 1: 23-25.

36. See August Wünsche, *Pesikta des Rab Kahana* (Leipzig: Otto Schulze, 1885), 2: 14a.

37. H. L. Ginsberg, *Legends of the Jews* (Philadelphia, 1946), 4: 339 and 6: 427-28.

38. *Wayikra Rabbah* 18.2 quoted in Freedman, *Midrash Rabbah* (London, 1938), 4: 229.

39. Ibid, 4: 229.

40. Ginsberg, *Legends*, 6: 427-28.

41. Moses Gaster, *The Chronicle of Jerachmeel* (London: Royal Asiatic Society, 1899), 206-7.

42. Josephus, *Jewish Antiquities*, 6: 279 and 281.

43. *2 Abot de Rabbi Nathan* 17, 37 quoted in Ginsberg, *Legends*, 6: 428.

44. This statement is in direct opposition to Josephus, who characterizes Jehoiachin as "being kind and just." See Josephus, *Jewish Antiquities*, 6: 211 and 213.

45. *2 Abot de Rabbi Nathan* 17, 38 quoted in Ginsberg, *Legends*, 6: 380.

46. *2 Targum Esther* 1.1 quoted in Freedman, *Midrash Rabbah*, 9: 33. "R. Tanhuma said: 'Nebuchadnezzar, may he be crushed and exterminated, amassed all the money in the world, and he was very niggardly with it. So when he felt his end approaching, he said to himself: 'Why should I leave all this money to Evil-Merodach?' So he ordered big ships of brass to be made, and filled them with money and dug trenches and hid them by the Euphrates and turned the waters of the Euphrates over them."

47. Grayson, *Assyrian and Babylonian Chronicles*, chron. 5, 102.

48. Ibid.

49. Josephus, *Against Apion*, 1: 156-58: "Under King Ithobal, Nabuchodonosor besieged Tyre for thirteen years."

50. Josephus, *Jewish Antiquities*, 6:217 and 219.

51. See J. P. Pritchard, *Ancient Near Eastern Texts Related to the Old Testament* (Princeton, 1955), 308.

52. See above, n. 9.

53. See Wiseman, *Chronicles*, 31ff., and Grayson, *Assyrian and Babylonian Chronicles*, 101.

54. The translation used here is by Dr. Gordon Newby of M. J. deGoeje et al. eds., *Annales* (Leiden, 1881-1882) prima series, vol. 2: 671.

55. See the discussions of the *Verse Account* (chap. 2) and *Prayer of Nabonidus* (chap. 3).

56. See Charles C. Torrey, *The Lives of the Prophets* (=*Journal of Biblical Literature Monograph Series*, vol. 1) (Philadelphia, 1946), 38-39.

Chapter 5. Nebuchadnezzar the Builder

1. See Joan Oates, *Babylon* (London: Thames & Hudson, 1979), 144. This is not to say the German excavators found nothing in the lowest levels at Babylon. Through a lucky coincidence, Koldewey excavated for a brief season the lower Old Babylonian levels at Babylon and found cuneiform texts. See also the work of Eckhard Unger, *Babylon die heilige Stadt nach der Beschreibung der Babylonier* (Berlin and Leipzig, 1931), 229-37, 240-45.

2. See discussion in Introduction, 19-20.

3. Oates, *Babylon*,148. See also D. J. Wiseman, *Nebuchadrezzar and Babylon* (Oxford: Oxford University Press, 1985), 53: "The northern city wall and gates had to be protected by a new outer and moat wall of burnt brick to replace the earlier escarpment of mud brick." A quay was constructed on the bank of the Euphrates to enable the loading and unloading of goods. Nabopolassar had begun the work on the moat wall, and Nebuchadnezzar finished the project. See Ibid, 51.

4. Stephen Langdon, *Building Inscriptions of the Neo Babylonian Empire*, I (Paris, 1905), in Oates, *Babylon*, 149.

5. Wiseman, *Nebuchadrezzar and Babylon*, 57.

6. Langdon, *Building Inscriptions*, in Oates, *Babylon*, 145.

7. See above, chap. 2, 26-27.

8. See Wiseman, *Nebucharrezzar and Babylon,* 42.

9. Ibid, 55.

10. See Stanley M. Burstein, *The Babyloniaca of Berossus* (=*Sources from the Ancient Near East*, vol. 1, fasc. 5) (Malibu: Undena Publications, 1978), 27.

11. Herodotus, *The Histories*, trans. Aubrey de Slincourt (Baltimore: Penguin Books, 1962), bk. 1: 179.

12. See H. T. Peck, *Harper's Dictionary of Classical Antiquities* (New York: American Book Co., 1896), 1438 and "Semiramis," in Cary and Denniston, *The Oxford Classical Dictionary* (Oxford: The Clarendon Press, 1966), 824.

13. Herodotus, *The Histories*, bk. 1: 185-89.

14. See Samuel K. Eddy, *The King is Dead: Studies in Near Eastern Resistance to Hellenism* 334-31 B.C. (Lincoln: University of Nebraska Press, 1961), 12.

15. Ibid, 121.

16. Ibid, 122-23: "In the Makedonian edition Ninos, husband-to-be of Semiramis, attacks a king of Baktria named Oxyartes. This man has the same name as the Baktrian nobleman of Alexander's time. Semiramis actually fights in this campaign. She stealthily leads a detachment of Ninos' army up a narrow ravine to capture

Oxyartes' army on the heights it is holding, as Alexander led an agile contingent of his army up a rocky defile to surprise the Baktrian forces entrenched on a high place. Then, in both the "Semiramis Legend" and the Alexander history, the principal person either marries or arranges a marriage in Baktria. Semiramis with Ninos and Alexander with Roxane. The hero then erects a monument on the Jaxartes River attesting an advance to the outermost rim of the civilized world. Furthermore, Semiramis, having become sole ruler after the death of Ninos, visits the Oracle of Ammon in Egypt, and receives the pronouncement that she will achieve undying fame. Her campaign against India takes on the colouring of Alexander's, since the Mesopotamians construct a bridge and river fleet on the Indus with the help of Kyprian and Phoenician sailors and shipwrights as the Makedonians actually did. Having been forced to retreat from India, Semiramis travels through Gedrosia, is conspired against in Babylon, and decides to die. She vanishes to the gods, much as Alexander returned to his father Ammon."

17. See Diodorus Siculus, *Universal History* in *Diodorus of Sicily*, trans. C. H. Oldfather (Cambridge, Mass.: Harvard University Press, 1933), 1:371ff.

18. Eddy, *The King Is Dead,* 123.

19. Ibid, 123.

20. Wiseman, *Nebuchadrezzar and Babylon*, 43.

21. Ibid, 55

22. Ibid.

23. Ibid.

24. Ibid, 63. It should be noted here that Wiseman's translation does not have universal acceptance. See W. von Soden, *Akkadisches Handwörterbuch* (Wiesbaden, 1974), 1120b (šabu = "taumelig werden.")

25. Ibid, 56-57.

26. Ibid, 57-59.

27. Amytis, the daughter of the king of Media, who became Nebuchadnezzar's wife.

28. Berossus, *Babyloniaca*, bk. 3, in Burstein, *The Babyloniaca of Berossus*, 27 and n. 106: "In describing the Hanging Gardens, one of the traditional wonders of the world. . . Berossus was catering to the interests of his Greek readers. His account probably reflects Babylonian popular tradition and not a written source since a very similar story about their origin occurred in the history of Alexander written by Cleitarchus of Alexandria."

29. Diodorus Siculus, *Universal History*, 1:385 and 387.

30. See Stephen Langdon, *Die neubabylonischen Königsinschriften, Vorderasiatische Bibliothek* vol. 4 (Leipzig, J. Hinrichs Buchhandlung, 1912), 76 iv 12.

31. Ibid, 126 iii 11.

32. Ibid, 126 iii 11.

33. See T. Pinches, "A Selection from the Miscellaneous Inscriptions of Assyria and Babylonia," in *The Cuneiform Inscriptions of Western Asia*, vol. 5 (London, 1880), 33 iii 12.

34. Langdon, *Die neubabylonischen Königsinschriften*, 186 iii 93.

35. Wiseman, *Nebuchadrezzar and Babylon,* 68.

36. Ibid, 67.

37. Herodotus, *The Histories*, bk. 1: 179. Nothing remains of the temple tower of Babylon now. In fact it is a big hole in the ground since the bricks were dug out years ago and dumped elsewhere.

38. Diodorus Siculus, *Universal History*, 1: 371 and 373.

39. See discussion above, chap. 2. See also the recently published work of Paul-Alain Beaulieu, *The Reign of Nabonidus, King of Babylon* (556-539 B.C.) (New Haven: Yale University Press, 1989).

40. See A. K. Grayson and Donald Redford, *Papyrus and Tablet* (Englewood Cliffs: Prentice Hall, 1973), 126-27.

41. Ibid, 118.

42. See James B. Pritchard, ed., *The Ancient Near East* (Princeton: Princeton University Press, 1975), 108ff.

43. See the discussion below, chap. 6.

Chapter 6. The "Myth" of Nebuchadnezzar

1. See above, 27. Reference to Nabonidus is also made in the so-called *Cyrus Cylinder* in which it says, "Nabonidus, the king who did not revere Marduk, he handed over to Cyrus." See the translation in A. K. Grayson and Donald Redford, *Papyrus and Tablet* (New Jersey: Prentice Hall, 1973), 124.

2. See discussion above, chap. 3.

3. Herodotus is a case in point. For discussions of his approaches, see Aubrey de Sélincourt, *The World of Herodotus* (Boston: Little, Brown & Co., 1962) and the essay by J. B. Bury in *Ancient Greek Historians* (New York: Dover Publications, 1958), 36ff. See also W. Baumgartner, "Herodotus babylonische und assyrische Nachrichten" (=*Archiv Orientainí* 18, 102, 1950) 69-106.

4. Herodotus says "Babylon lies in a wide plain, a vast city in the form of a square with sides nearly fourteen miles long and a circuit of some fifty-six miles, and in addition to its enormous size it surpassed in splendour any city of the known world. It is surrounded by a broad deep moat full of water, and within the moat there is a wall fifty royal cubits wide and two hundred high." From here he proceeds (1: 179-85) to outline the features of the ziqqurat of Bel and the inner walls as well as the diverting of the course of the Euphrates, all of which is associated with Semiramis.

5. There are numerous references to the "superhuman" feats of the Cyclopes in Pausanias, *Description of Greece* (London: William Heinemann 1954), bk. 7. 25. 3-6 and elsewhere. "Though the Argives could not take the wall of Mycenae by storm, built as it was like the wall of Tiryns by the Cyclopes, as they were called, yet the Mycenaeans were forced to leave their city through lack of provisions." See J. G. Frazer, *Pausanias's Description of Greece* (New York: Biblo & Tannen, 1965).

6. See "Semiramis," in George Wissowa, *Realencyclopaedie der classischen Altertumswissenschaft* (J. D. Metzherrscher Verlag, 1940), Supp. 7: 1203ff.

7. Cory, *Ancient Fragments,* 71. Compare this account with Nebuchadnezzar's own inscriptions. See Wiseman, *Chronicles,* 65ff, Pritchard, *Ancient Near Eastern Texts,* 307ff. and Berger, *Die neubabylonischen Königsinschriften,* 64ff., 84ff.

8. Cory, *Ancient Fragments,* 72ff. This is preserved (through Abydenus by Eusebius) in *Praeparatio Evangelica* 10.

9. See Cory, *Ancient Fragments,* 90ff.

10. See above, 43.   See also P. Schnabel, *Berossos und die babylonisch-hellenistische Literatur* (Hildesheim, 1969) and Robert Drews, "The Babylonian Chronicles and Berossus," *Iraq* 37 (1975): 52ff.

11. Cory, *Ancient Fragments,* 65, "After a short time, Nabuchodonosor (Nebuchadnezzar), receiving the intelligence of his father's death, set the affairs of Egypt and the other countries in order, and committed the captives he had taken from the Jews and Phoenicians and Syrians, and of the nations belonging to Egypt, to some of his friends, in order that they might conduct that part of his forces that had on heavy armor, together with the rest of his baggage, to Babylonia."

12. Ibid, 65-6.

13. See above. It is interesting to note that Aristotle (*Politics*) also indicates a fascination with the city of Babylon, because of its immense size.

14. Regarding the nature of Berossus's *Babyloniaca,* see Drews, "Babylonian Chronicles," 52-5.

15. See the discussion of Babylon and Semiramis above and chap. 5, ns. 25-27.

16. Syncellus and Eusebius preserve a fragment of Alexander Polyhistor concerning Belus (Cory, *Ancient Fragments,* 59ff.) that reveals the same attitude. He writes: "The person, who was supposed to have presided over them was a woman named Omoroca; which in the Chaldee language is Thalatth; which in Greek is interpreted Thalassa, the sea; but, according to the most true computation, it is equivalent to Selene, the moon. All things being in this situation, Belus came, and cut the woman asunder: and, out of one half of her, he formed the earth, and of the other half the heavens; and at the same time he destroyed the animals in the abyss. All this (he says) was an allegorical description of nature. For the whole universe consisting of moisture, and animals being continually generated therein; the deity (Belus), above-mentioned, cut off his own head; upon which the other gods mixed the blood, as it gushed out, with the earth; and from thence men were formed. On this account it is that men are rational, and partake of divine knowledge. This Belus, whom men call Dis (of Pluto) divided the darkness, and separated the heavens from the earth, and reduced the universe to order. But the animals so recently created, not being able to bear the prevalence of light, died.

Belus, upon this, seeing a vast space quite uninhabited, though by nature very fruitful, ordered one of the gods to take off his head; and when it was taken off, they were to mix the blood with the soil of the earth. . . .Belus also formed the stars, and the sun and the moon, together with the five planets."

This story of Belus clearly finds its antecedent in the *Enuma Elish* story, in which Marduk performs the same functions.

17. For the inscriptions of the Achaemenid kings, see F. H. Weissbach, *Die Keilinschriften der Achämeniden* (=*Vorderasiatische Bibliothek,* Heft 3) (Leipzig, 1911), and Borger, 3: 32ff.

18. See Pritchard, *Ancient Near Eastern Texts* (3d ed.) 315ff., Grayson, *Papyrus and Tablet* (New Jersey, Prentice Hall, 1973) 124. "But the god Marduk. . .took pity on the people of Sumer and Akkad who had become like corpses, he was appeased and had mercy. Carefully looking through all lands he sought an upright prince after his own heart. Taking him by the hand he pronounced his name: 'Cyrus, king of Anshan.' He designated him for rule over everything. At his feet he subdued the Qutu and all the Umman-manda. The black-headed people which Marduk had allowed him to conquer he always administered in truth and justice. The god Marduk, the

great lord, a guardian of his people, looked with joy upon his good works and upright heart. He commanded him to march to his city Babylon."

19. See above, chap. 3 and Ibid, 120. "The seventh year of Nabonidus: The king was in the city Tema while the prince, Belshazzar, his officers and his army remained in Babylonia. The king did not come to Babylon in the month Nisan, the God Nab did not come to Babylon, Marduk did not come out, and the New Year's festival was cancelled."

20. Ibid, 136.

21. Ibid, 121. For a discussion of Nabonidus and his relationship to the Hebrew sources, see above, Chap. 6, 170ff. Such a picture had to combine historicity with folkloristic elements embodied in other sources.

See John J. Collins, *The Apocalyptic Visions of the Book of Daniel*, in F. M. Cross, ed., *Harvard Semitic Monographs*, vol. 16 (Missoula: Scholars Press, 1977), 88f.: "The dating of Daniel 7-12 to the time of Antiochus Epiphanes is of basic importance for the analysis of the composition of the book, since the tales in Daniel 1-6 do not reflect the same historical situation and must have originally been independent of the later chapters." Collins then suggests (8-11) that the tales contained in Daniel 2-6 do not refer to Antiochus and were probably not written in Maccabean times. Again, a relationship to Nabonidus is proposed.

22. In discussing the Hebrew sources, reference will be made (when appropriate) to Josephus's *Jewish Antiquities* and Jerome's commentaries on Daniel and Isaiah. Because both authors include essentially midrashic material in their works, it seems best to treat their contents here.

For a recent treatment of Jewish historiography and its relationship to folklore and legend, see John Van Seters, "Histories and Historians of the Ancient Near East: The Israelites," in *Orientalia* (Nova Series) 50 (1981): 137ff.

23. References to the power of Babylon in the Old Testament (particularly in Daniel) are used for entirely different purposes than they are in the Hellenic sources. The strength of Yahweh could best evidence itself in opposition to the "mighty Babylon" and its haughty king Nebuchadnezzar, who is characterized as a boastful monarch who, nevertheless, would be brought to his knees (Daniel 4).

24. The bibliography on this subject is understandably immense. As early as 1708, H. van der Hart attempted to identify the "four kingdoms" referred to in Daniel. See *De quatuor monarchiis Babyloniae pro antiquae historiae judaicae luce ad illustrandum Colossum in insomnio Nebuchadnezaris Danii* (1708), 15ff. See also his *Danielis quatuor animalisa, non quatuor monarchiarum fabula, sed quatuor regum Babylon's Nebuchadnezaris, Evilmerodachi, Belsazaris et Cyri, historia*, (1710), 18ff. This work was taken up by Harenberg in *Die Aufklärung des Buches Daniel*, 304ff.

25. Some scholars have tried to identify historical figures with each of the four kingdoms. After the discovery and translation of cuneiform documents, there were attempts to associate Nebuchadnezzar, Amel Marduk, Neriglissar, and Nabonidus with them. See, for example, P. Riessler, *Das Buch Daniel erklärt in kurzgefassten wissenschaftlicher Commentar* (1902), 17ff., 68ff., in which he tried to associate the Nebuchadnezzar tradition with Nabonidus and identified the four kingdoms with the reigns of Nabonidus, Belshazzar, Cyrus, and Darius the Mede (i.e., Cambyses).

Other scholars have tried to stress (what they believe) the purely folkloristic nature of the Book of Daniel. See, for example, Holscher, *Die Entstehung des Buches Daniel* (1919), 113ff. in which the author asserts that it contains many folktales, for which parallels can be found in other bodies of folk literature and legends. See also

Kuhl, "Die Drei Männer im Feuer" in *Zeitschrift für die alttestamentiliche Wissenschaft* Beih. 55 (1930), and Baumgartner, *Das Buch Daniel* (1926) in which the stories are called "orientalische Hofsgeschichten" similar to tales in the *1001 Nights*. See the article of von Soden, "Eine babylonische Volksüberlieferung von Nabonid in den Danielerzählungen" in *Zeitschrift für die alttestamentliche Wissenschaft* 53 (1935), 83ff.

26. von Soden, "Eine babylonische Volksüberlieferung," 83ff.

27. See A. Leo Oppenheim, *The Interpretation of Dreams in the Ancient Near East* (=*Transactions of the American Philosophical Society*, vol. 436, pt. 3) (Philadelphia, 1956): 250. See also Joan Oates, *Babylon* (London: Thames Hudson, 1979), 132-33.

28. Grayson, *Papyrus and Tablet*, 118. For an analysis of the contents of the dreams of Nabonidus, as well as their relationship to other ancient Near Eastern and Hellenic texts, see Oppenheim, *Interpretation of Dreams*, 192ff. The fragmentary dreams, as well as the interesting text in which Nebuchadnezzar appears, may have related to Nabonidus's attention to Sin as well.

29. See H. H. Schaeder, *Ezra der Schreiber* (=*Beiträge zur historischen Theologie* (Tubingen, Mohr, 1930) for further commentary.

30. See above, chap. 3.

31. *The Wisdom of Ahiqar* in Charles, 2: 754.

32. See above, chap. 3.

33. See above, chap. 1.

34. von Soden, "Eine babylonische Volksüberlieferung," 88-9. See also the interesting article by Baumgartner, "Neues keilschriftliches Material zum Buche Daniel?" in *Zeitschrift für die alttestamentliche Wissenschaft* 44: 42ff.

35. The question should be raised as to why the name of Sennecherib is not associated with such a characterization. Although the *Talmud* (in the tractates *Sanhedrin* and *Megillah*) and the midrashim repeatedly mention him (along with Nebuchadnezzar) as one of "two wicked men, two destroyers," he never appears as frequently as does his Chaldean counterpart. Von Soden, "Eine babylonische Volksüberlieferung," (87-89) may have already suggested the reason for this. Although the besieging of Jerusalem is an act worthy of note, only Nebuchadnezzar deported captives. At the end of the Exilic period, the Hebrews returned to Palestine with the memory of the destruction and a knowledge of the events of the neo-Babylonian period. Hence, although both kings are referred to in *Numbers Rabbah* as "sovereigns of the universe" and "lords of the world" (21:34; 23:14), Nebuchadnezzar's acts and the portrayal of Nabonidus in the cuneiform sources better related to the *function* of the commentary.

The "universality" of the Nebuchadnezzar image can be seen in the *Apocrypha*. Mention has been made of the books in which his name appears (see above, 71). The Book of Judith, while describing Nebuchadnezzar as one "who reigned over the Assyrians in Nineveh" nevertheless relates details that can only apply to the Seleucid period. Charles, in his commentary on the nature of the work itself (1: 245-46), indicates the difficulty in associating its contents with any specific point in time ("Such being the method of the book, we need not expect to identify all the geographical any more than the personal names"). As was the case with the Book of Daniel, Tobit, Judith, and other apocryphal and pseudoepigraphical texts were intended to know no limit in time or space; everything from an association of Nebuchadnezzar with Nineveh to a conquest of Ethiopia and Persia could be applicable to any age and any individual.

There has long been (likewise) a question as to the time of the authorship of Daniel 2-4 (written in Aramaic). Some have related it to the third century B.C. and the time of Antiochus IV Epiphanes; others see it differently. For a discussion of this material, see Hartman, *Book of Daniel,* 154ff., 168ff.

36. *Lamentations Rabbah* II, 10:14.

37. Ibid, 23.

38. *Esther Rabbah* 1: 19. It is also here that Nebuchadnezzar is called "the foremost of ravagers" (*Proem* 10).

39. *Lamentations Rabbah* 2: 10:14. In *Numbers Rabbah* 1:24 there is mention of his dwelling place as having been with the beasts of the field. "He further told him: 'You said that there were none among all the inhabitants of the world good enough for you to dwell among, but it is you who are not good enough to dwell among them.'"

The foolish pride of Nebuchadnezzar is stressed repeatedly in *Midrash Rabbah* (as it is in Daniel 3-4). In *Numbers Rabbah* 20:1 we read "He raised up Solomon as king over Israel and over the whole earth, and he did the same with Nebuchadnezzar. The former built the Temple and uttered numerous songs and supplications, while the latter destroyed it and reviled and blasphemed, saying: 'I will ascend above the heights of the clouds; I will be like the Most High.'"

Like the midrashim, Jerome, in his *Commentary on Daniel,* emphasizes the pride and wealth of the Chaldeans by contrasting it with the attitude of the Hebrews in captivity. "The Hebrews question why Daniel and the three lads did not enter before the king along with other wise men, and why they were ordered to be slain with the rest when the decree was issued. They have explained (the difficulty) in this way, that at that time, when the king was promising rewards and gifts and the greatest honor, they were unwilling (to go before him) lest they should appear to be shamelessly grasping after the wealth and honor of the Chaldeans" (*PL* 25:499 and *CCSL* 75 A, 786, I. 203-11). See Jay Baverman, *Jerome's Commentary on Daniel: A Study of Comparative Jewish and Christian Interpretations of the Hebrew Bible* (=*Catholic Biblical Quarterly Monograph Series* no. 7) (Washington: Catholic Biblical Association of America, 1978), 77. Baverman cites sixteen "traditions" in the writings of Jerome, some of which have no parallel in rabbinic literature or in the other commentaries on Daniel (from Hippolytus, 140-235). As Jerome himself says, "I have made it my resolve to make available for Latin readers the hidden treasures of Hebrew erudition and the recondite teachings of the Masters of the Synagogue, as long as these things are in keeping with the Holy Scriptures" (*PL* 25:1455).

Josephus, while including extensive sections from the Book of Daniel in his *Jewish Antiquities,* also occasionally adds midrashic material to his work. For a commentary on his sources, see Harold W. Attridge, *The Interpretation of Biblical History in the Antiquitates Judaicae of Flavius Josephus* (=*Harvard Dissertations in Religion* 7) (Missoula: Scholars Press, 1976).

Finally, mention should be made of the comments of Jerachmeel on the "insanity" of Nebuchadnezzar. In addition to his reference to the king's behavior in Babylon (see above, 68), he includes the following in his *Chronicle*: "Nebuchadnezzar did not actually change in his body or assume other than human form, but his sight and his mind and language were all transformed. Other men saw him as an ox to his navel and as a lion from his navel to his feet. The food he ate was the herbs that human beings eat, to show that in the beginning he chewed like an ox but in the end was like a lion to slay all wicked men." These words are reminiscent of the *Lives of the Prophets* quoted previously. See above, chap. 3, and Micha Joseph Bin Gorion, *Mimekor Yisrael* (Bloomington: University of Indiana Press, 1976), 1: 201.

Chapter 7. Concluding Remarks

1. See Pausanias, *Description of Greece* (London: William Heinemann, 1954), bk. 8: 25, 3-6.

2. See discussion above, chap. 1.

3. Herodotus, *The Histories*, trans. Aubrey de Sélincourt (Baltimore: Penguin Books, 1962), bk. 1: 179-85.

4. See above, chap. 6.

5. See *Diodorus of Sicily*, trans. C. H. Oldfather (Cambridge, Mass.: Harvard University Press, 1933), 1: 371, 373.

6. See *The Chronicles of Jerachmeel*, trans. Moses Gaster (New York: Ktav Publishing House, 1971), bk. 66: 1-2.

Bibliography:
Suggestions for Further Reading

Cuneiform Sources

Albright, W. F. "The Conquests of Nabonidus in Arabia." *Journal of the Royal Asiatic Society* (1925): 293-95.

Baumgartner, W. "Herodots babylonische und assyrische Nachrichten." *Archiv Orientalní* 18-12 (1950): 69-106.

Beaulieu, Paul-Alain. *The Reign of Nabonidus, King of Babylon* (556-539 B.C.). New Haven: Yale University Press, 1989.

Berger, R. P. *Die neubabylonischen Königsinschriften (Alter Orient und Altes Testament* 4/1. Neukirchen-Vluyn, 1973).

Borger, R. "Der Aufstieg des neubabylonischen Reiches." *Journal of Cuneiform Studies* (1965).

Brinkman, J. A. "The Early Neo-Babylonian Monarchy." *Le palais et la royauté*, edited by P. Garelli, 409-15. Paris: Geuthner, 1974.

————. *Prelude to Empire. Occasional Publications of the Babylonian Fund* 7. Philadelphia, 1984.

Burstein, S. M. *The Babyloniaca of Berossus. Sources from the Ancient Near East*, 1/5. Malibu: Undena Publications, 1978.

Cooke, G. A. *A Textbook of North Semitic Inscriptions*. Oxford, 1903.

Dandamayev, M. *Rabstvo v. Vavilonii*. Moscow, 1975.

Delitzsch, F. *Die babylonische Chronik*. Leipzig, 1906.

Dougherty, R. P. "A Babylonian City in Arabia." *American Journal of Archaeology* 34 (1930): 296-312.

————. *Nabonidus and Belshazzar.* =*Yale Oriental Series, Researches* 15. New Haven, 1929.

————. "Nabonidus in Arabia." *Journal of the American Oriental Society* 42 (1922): 305-16.

————. "Tema's Place in the Egypto-Babylonian World of the Sixth Century B.C." *Mizraim* 1 (1933): 140-43.

Drews, Robert. "The Babylonian Chronicles and Berossus." *Iraq* 37 (1975): 52ff.

Eddy, S. K. *The King is Dead: Studies in Near Eastern Resistance to Hellenism* 334-31 B.C. Lincoln: University of Nebraska Press, 1961.

Gadd, C. J. "The Harran Inscriptions of Nabonidus." *Anatolian Studies* 8 (1958): 35-92.

Grayson, A. K. *Babylonian and Assyrian Chronicles. Texts from Cuneiform Sources* 5. Locust Valley; J. J. Augistin, 1975.

Grayson, A. K. and D. Redford. *Papyrus and Tablet.* Prentice Hall, 1973.

Komoroczy, G. "Berossus and the Mesopotamian Literature." *Acta Antiqua Academiae Scientiarum Hungaricae* 29 (1973): 125-52.

_____. "Ein assyrischer König in der arabischen Überlieferung." *Altorientalische Forschungen* 1 (1974): 153-64.

Lambert, W. G. *The Background of the Jewish Apocalyptic.* London: Athlone Press, 1978.

_____. "Berossus and Babylonian Eschatology." *Iraq* 38 (1976): 31-3.

_____. "Nebuchadnezzar, King of Justice." *Iraq* 27 (1965): 1-11.

_____. "A New Source for the Reign of Nabonidus." *Archiv für Orientforschung* 22 (1968/69): 1-8.

Landsberger, B. and Th. Bauer. "Zu neuveröffentlichen Geschichtsquellen der Zeit von Assarhaddon bis Nabonid." *Zeitschrift für Assyriologie* 37 (1927): 61-98.

Lane, W. H. *Babylonian Problems.* London: John Murray, 1923.

Langdon, S. *Die neubabylonischen Königsinschriften. Vorderasiatische Bibliothek,* vol. 4. Leipzig: J. Hinrichs Buchhandlung, 1912.

Lewy, J. "The Late Assyro-Babylonian Cult of the Moon and its Culmination at the Time of Nabonidus." *Hebrew Union College Annual* 19 (1946): 405-89.

Milik, J. T. "Priere de Nabonide." *Revue biblique* 63 (1956): 407-15.

Moran, W. L. "Notes on the New Nabonidus Inscriptions." *Orientalia* n.s. 28 (1958): 130-40.

Neusner, J. *A History of the Jews in Babylonia,* vol. 3. Leiden: Brill, 1968.

Oates, J. *Babylon.* London: Thames & Hudson, 1979.

Olmstead, A. T. E. "Assyrian Historiography." *University of Missouri Studies, Social Science Series* 3.1 (1916): 1-66.

_____. "The Chaldean Dynasty." *Hebrew Union College Annual* 2 (1925): 29-55.

Ravn, O.E. *Herodotus' Description of Babylon.* Copenhagen, 1942.

Röllig, W. "Erwägungen zu neuen Stelen König Nabonidus." *Zeitschrift für Assyriologie* 56 (1964): 218-60.

_____. "Nabonid und Tema." *Compte rendus de la rencontre assyriologique internationale* 11 (1964): 21-32.

Roux, G. *Ancient Iraq.* Baltimore: Penguin Books, 1980.

Sack, R. H. *Amel-Marduk, 562-560 B.C. Alter Orient und Altes Testament,* Sonderreihe, vol. 4. Neukirchen Vluyn, 1972.

_____. "Nebuchadnezzar and Nabonidus in Folklore and History." *Mesopotamia* 17 (1982): 67-131.

Saggs, H. W. F. *The Greatness that was Babylon.* London: Sidgwick and Jackson, 1962.

Segall B. "The Arts and King Nabonidus." *American Journal of Archaeology* 59 (1955): 315-18.

Smith, Sidney. *Babylonian Historical Texts Relating to the Capture and Downfall of Babylon.* London, 1924.

———. *Isaiah Chapters XL-LV: Schweich Lectures of the British Academy* (1940). Oxford, 1944.

Tadmor, H.   "Inscriptions of Nabonaid: Historical Arrangement." *Assyriological Studies* 16 (Chicago, 1965).

Unger, Eckhard. *Babylon, die heilige Stadt nach der Beschreibung der Babylonier.* Berlin and Leipzig, 1931.

Van Beek, G. W. "Frankincense and Myrrh." *Biblical Archaeologist Reader* 12 (New York, 1964).

Van Seters, John. *In Search of History.* New Haven: Yale University Press, 1983.

Vogelstein, M.   "Nebuchadnezzar's Reconquest of Phoenicia and Palestine and the Oracles of Ezekiel." *Hebrew Union College Annual* 23 (1950-51): 2: 197-220.

Weidner E. "Hochverrat gegen Nebukadnezar II." *Archiv für Orientforschung* 17 (1954-56): 1-9.

Weinfeld, M.   "Cult Centralization in Israel in the Light of a Neo-Babylonian Analogy." *Journal of Near Eastern Studies* 23 (1964): 202-12.

Weisberg, D.   *Guild Structure and Political Allegiance in Early Achaemenid Mesopotamia.* New Haven, 1967.

Wetzel, F. "Babylon zur Zeit Herodotus." *Zeitschrift für Assyriologie* (n.f. 14, 1944): 45-68.

Wiseman, D. *Chronicles of Chaldean Kings (626-556 B.C.).* London, 1956.

Zawadzki, S.   *The Fall of Assyria and Median-Babylonian Relations in Light of the Nabopolassar Chronicle.* Poznan, 1988.

Classical, Hebrew and Arabic Sources

Attridge,H. W. *The Interpretation of Biblical History in the Antiquitates Judaicae of Flavius Josephus.* =*Harvard Dissertations in Religion* 7 Missoula, 1976.

Bowker, J. *The Targums and Rabbinic Literature.* Cambridge, 1969.

Braude, W. G. *Peskta Rabbati.* New Haven, 1968.

Collins, J. J.   *The Apocalyptic Visions of the Book of Daniel.* In *Harvard Semitic Monographs* vol. 16, edited by F. Cross. Missoula, 1977.

Cory, I. *Ancient Fragments of the Phoenician, Chaldean, Egyptian, Tyrian, Carthaginian, Indian, Persian and Other Writers.* London, 1876.

de Slincourt, A. *The World of Herodotus.* Boston, 1962.

Drews, R. "The Babylonian Chronicles and Berossus." *Iraq* 37 (1975): 52ff.

Eddy, S. K. *The King is Dead: Studies in Near Eastern Resistance to Hellenism 334-31 B.C.* Lincoln, 1961.

Eusebius Pamphili. *Eusebii Chronicorum Libri Duo.* edited by A. Schöne. Berlin, 1866.

Flavius Josephus.   *The Works of Flavius Josephus* translated by Ralph Marcus. Cambridge, 1937.

Ginsberg, H. L. *The Legends of the Jews.* Philadelphia, 1946.

Hartman, L. F. *The Book of Daniel.* =*Anchor Bible*, vol. 23. Garden City, 1978.

Helm, R. *Die griechischen christlichen Schriftsteller der ersten Jahrhunderte, Eusebius' Werke* vol. 7. Berlin, 1956.

Hieronymi. *Presbyteri Opera Commentarium en Danielem* II Visio 5 in *Corpus Christianorum, Series Latina*. Turnholti, 1964.

————. *Presbyteri Opera Commentarium en Esaiam* V, Visio 14, 19 in *Corpus Christianorum, Series Latina*. Turnholti, 1964.

Hitti, P. *History of the Arabs*. London, 1961.

Jacoby, F. *Fragmenta der griechischen Historiker*. Leiden, 1964.

Karst, J. *Eusebius' Werke V, Die Chronik aus dem Armenischen übersetzt*. Leipzig, 1911.

Komoroczy, G. "Berosos and the Mesopotamian Literature." *Acta Antiqua* 21 (1973): 125ff.

————. "Ein assyrischer König in der arabischen Überlieferung." *Altorientalische Forschungen* 1 (1974): 153-64.

Kuhrt, A. and S. Sherwin-White, eds. *Hellenism in the East =Hellenistic Culture and Society*, 2. Berkeley, 1987.

Lambert, W. G. *The Background of Jewish Apocalyptic*. London, 1978.

Lofgren, O. "An Arabic Recension of the Vitae Prophetarium." *Orientalia Suecana* 25-27: 77-105.

Mandelbaum, B., ed. *Pesikta de Rab Kahana*. New York, 1962.

Mosshammer, A. A. *The Chronicle of Eusebius and the Greek Chronographic Tradition*. Lewisburg, Pa., 1979.

Müller. *Fragmenta Historicorum Graecorum*. Paris, 1848.

Richter, J. *Berosi Chaldaeorum Historiae*. Lipsiae, 1825.

Rowley, H. H. *Darius the Mede*. New York, 1964.

Schaeder, H. H. *Ezra der Schreiber. Beiträge zur historischen Theologie*. Tubingen, 1930.

Schaff, P., and H. Wace. *A Select Library of the Nicene and Post Nicene Fathers of the Christian Church*. Grand Rapids, 1961.

Schnabel, P. *Berossus und die babylonisch-hellenistische Literatur*. Hildesheim, 1968.

Schürer, E. *A History of the Jewish People in the Age of Jesus Christ* translated by G. Vermes and F. Millar. Edinburg, 1973.

Thackeray, H. St. John. *Josephus, the Man and the Historian*. New York, 1929.

Thompson, J. W. *A History of Historical Writing*. New York, 1942.

Van Seters, J. "Histories and Historians of the Ancient Near East: the Israelites." *Orientalia* n.s. 50 (1981): 137ff.

————. *In Search of History*. New Haven, 1983.

Vermes, G. *The Dead Sea Scrolls in English*. Baltimore, 1962.

Wachholder, B. Z. *Eupolemus—A Study of Judaeo Greek Literature*. Cincinnati, 1974.

Xenophon. *Cyropaedia*. Translated by T. E. Page and W. H. D. Rouse. London, 1912.

Index